Top Tips
from the
Baby Whisperer:
Potty Training

Top Tips from the Baby Whisperer: Potty Training

Tracy Hogg
with Melinda Blau

Vermilion
LONDON

3 5 7 9 10 8 6 4 2

Published in 2010 by Vermilion, an imprint of Ebury Publishing

Ebury Publishing is a Random House Group company

Copyright © Tracy Hogg and Melinda Blau 2005

Tracy Hogg and Melinda Blau have asserted their right to be identified as the authors of this Work in accordance with the Copyright, Designs and Patents Act 1988

The Random House Group Limited Reg. No. 954009

Addresses for companies within the Random House Group can be found at
www.randomhouse.co.uk

Mixed Sources
Product group from well-managed
forests and other controlled sources
www.fsc.org Cert no. TT-COC-2139
© 1996 Forest Stewardship Council

A CIP catalogue record for this book is available from the British Library
The Random House Group Limited supports The Forest Stewardship Council (FSC),
the leading international forest certification organisation. All our titles that are printed on
Greenpeace approved FSC certified paper carry the FSC logo. Our paper procurement policy
can be found at www.rbooks.co.uk/environment

Printed and bound in Great Britain by CPI Mackays, Chatham ME5 8TD

ISBN 9780091929756

Text previously published in *The Baby Whisperer Solves All Your Problems*

Copies are available at special rates for bulk orders. Contact the sales development team
on 020 7840 8487 for more information.

To buy books by your favourite authors and register for offers, visit www.rbooks.co.uk

Contents

Introduction

I have always been proud of my ability to help parents understand and care for their young children and I feel honoured whenever a family asks me into its life. It's a very intimate and rewarding experience. Since I published my first two books (now some years ago), I've had a series of adventures and surprises that go beyond anything I could have imagined as a girl in Yorkshire.

I've travelled around the country and the world and met some of the most wonderful parents and children, who've opened their homes and hearts to me. I've spoken to thousands more via my website, reading and responding to their emails and joining them in my chat rooms. I've received many letters of thanks and confirmation from mums and dads who have followed my advice. But I've also been inundated with requests for help.

Maybe you're trying to get your baby on a structured routine, as I suggest, but you're not sure whether the same principles apply to eight-month-olds as to newborns. Maybe you're confused about why your child isn't doing what other children are doing. Or maybe you're faced with a deeply entrenched problem – a feeding difficulty, or a child who isn't potty trained. Whatever the dilemma, your anguished refrain is almost always the same: 'Where do I begin, Tracy? What do I do first?' And then, 'Why do some of your strategies seem not to work with my child?'

I've been fielding such questions for several years now and consulted on some extremely difficult cases. So now, in this book, I want to take your hand, ease your fears and show you how to empower yourself as a parent. I want to teach you what I've learned from a lifetime of baby whispering; I want to teach you how to think like me.

When parents come to me with a particular challenge, to assess what's really going on in that household and with that baby or toddler, I always ask at least one, if not a string of questions, both about the child and about what parents have done so far in response to their situation. Then I can come up with a proper plan of action.

My goal with this book is to help you understand my thought process and get you in the habit of asking questions for yourself. In time, you, too, will not only be a baby whisperer but an ace problem solver in your own right.

As you read on, however, I want you to remember this important point: a problem is nothing more than an issue that needs to be addressed or a situation calling for a creative solution. Ask the right questions, and you'll come up with the right answers.

Tuning In

Baby whispering begins by observing, respecting and communicating with your baby. It means that you see your child for who she really is – her personality and her particular quirks – and you tailor your parenting strategies accordingly.

I've been told that I'm one of the few baby experts who takes the child's point of view. I've had new parents look at me like I'm crazy when I introduce myself to their four-day-old baby. And parents of older children positively gape at me when I 'translate' the mournful cries of their eight-month-old. I also translate 'banguage' (baby language) for parents, because it helps them remember that the little being in their arms, or the toddler tearing around the room, also has feelings and opinions.

How often have I witnessed a scene like this: a mother says

to her little boy, 'Now Billy, you don't want Adam's truck.' Poor little Billy doesn't talk yet but, if he did, I'd bet he'd say, 'Yes I do, Mum. Why else do you think I grabbed it away from Adam in the first place?' But Mum doesn't listen to him. She either takes the truck out of Billy's hand or tries to coax him into relinquishing it willingly. 'Be a good lad and give it back to him.' Well, at that point, I can almost count the seconds until meltdown! I'm not saying that, just because Billy wants the truck, he should be allowed to bully Adam – far from it. What I am saying is that we need to listen to our children, even when they say things we don't want to hear.

The same skills that I teach parents of infants – observing body language, listening to cries, slowing down so that you can really figure out what's going on – those skills are just as important as your baby grows into a toddler and beyond, and as you and your child face new challenges.

Throughout this book, I'll remind you of some of the techniques I've developed to help you tune in and take your time, particularly the acronym E.A.S.Y. (Eat, Activity, Sleep, and time for You – see Chapter 1).

I know firsthand that parenting is anything but 'E.A.S.Y.' It's particularly hard for new parents to know which end is up, especially sleep-starved new mums, but all parents need help.

I'm just trying to give you tools to use when you might not have your wits about you.

I also know that life just gets more complicated as babies become toddlers and as the family grows. My goal is to keep your baby on track and your own life on an even keel – or at least as even as it can be with young children underfoot. In the midst of a tussle with your child or children, it's easy to forget good advice and lapse into old patterns. I mean, how clearheaded can you be when your baby is screaming at the top of her lungs because her two-year-old brother, in the midst of supposedly learning how to use the toilet, decided that baby sister's head was as good a place as any to test out his new Magic Marker?

I can't be in each of your homes, but, if you have my handy little acronym in your head, maybe it will seem like I'm standing next to you, reminding you what to do. So here's another acronym for your parental bag of tricks: 'P.C.'

Be a 'P.C.' Parent

I don't mean politically correct; rather, a P.C. parent is patient and conscious, two qualities that will serve you well no matter how old your child is. Invariably, when I meet parents who are beset by a particular problem, my prescription always involves one, if not both, of these elements. But it's not just problems that require P.C. parenting; so do everyday interactions. Playtime, a trip to the toilet, being with other children and a host of other daily occurrences, are enhanced by Mum or Dad having a P.C. mind-set.

No parent is P.C. all the time but, the more we do it, the more it becomes a natural way of acting. We get better with practice.

Patience: it takes patience to parent well, because it's a hard, seemingly endless road, one that requires a long-term perspective. Today's Big Problem – whether it's encouraging your child to eat more vegetables or to use the potty – becomes a distant memory a month from now, but we tend to forget that when we're living through it. I've seen it happen time and again: parents who, in the heat of the moment, take what seems like an easier road, only to find out later that 'accidental parenting' leads them to a dangerous dead end.

Having a child can be messy and disorderly, too. Therefore, you also need patience (and internal fortitude) to tolerate at least the clutter, spills and finger marks, let alone the nappy, potty and toilet messes. Parents who don't will find it harder to get through their child's firsts. What toddler manages to drink from a real cup without first spilling pints of liquid on to the floor? Eventually, only a drizzle slips out the side of his mouth and then finally he gets most of it down, but it doesn't happen overnight, and it certainly doesn't happen without setbacks along the way. Allowing your child to master table skills, to learn how to pour or to wash himself, to let him walk around a living room filled with lots of no-nos – all of these things require parents' patience.

Parents who lack this important quality can unwittingly create obsessive behaviours even in very young children. Tara, a two-year-old I met in my travels, had obviously learned her lessons well from her ultra-neat mother, Cynthia. Walking into this mum's house, it was hard to tell a toddler lived there. And no wonder. Cynthia hovered constantly and followed her daughter around with a damp cloth, wiping her face, mopping up her spills, putting toys back into the toy box the moment Tara dropped them. Tara was already a chip off the old block: 'duhtee' was one of her first words. That might have been cute if it weren't for the fact that Tara was afraid to venture very far on her own and cried if other kids touched her.

We do our little ones an injustice when we don't allow

them to do what kids do: get a little dirty and get into a little mischief every now and then. A wonderful P.C. mum I met told me she regularly had 'Pig Night' with her children, a dinner without utensils. And here's a surprising irony: when we actually give our kids permission to go wild, they often don't stray as far as you think they will.

Patience is particularly critical when you're trying to change bad habits. Naturally, the older the child, the longer it takes. Regardless of age, though, you must accept that change takes time – you can't rush the process. But I will tell you this: it's easier to be patient now and to take the time to teach your children and tell them what you expect. After all, who would you rather ask to clean up after himself, a two-year-old or a teenager?

Consciousness: consciousness of who your child is should begin the moment she takes her first breath outside the womb. Always be aware of your child's perspective. I mean this both figuratively and literally: squat down to your child's eye level. See what the world looks like from her vantage point. Take a whiff of the air. Imagine what the smells are like to a baby's sensitive nose. Listen. How loud is the din of the crowd? Might it be a bit much for Baby's ears?

I'm not saying you should stay away from new places. On the

contrary, it's good to expose children to new sights, sounds and people. But, if your infant repeatedly cries in unfamiliar settings, as a conscious parent you'll know that she's telling you: 'It's too much. Please go slower' or 'Try this with me in another month.' Consciousness lets you tune in and, in time, allows you to get to know your child and trust your instincts about her.

Consciousness is also a matter of thinking things through before you do them, and planning ahead. Don't wait for disaster to strike, especially if you've been there before. For instance, if you see that your child and your best friend's child are constantly at war and the morning always ends in tears, arrange a play date with a different child and, when you want to go out for 'a jaw' with your best friend, get a baby-sitter.

Consciousness means paying attention to the things you say and what you do with and to your child – and being consistent. Inconsistencies confuse children. So if, one day, you say, 'No eating in the living room,' and the next night you ignore it, your words will eventually mean nothing. He'll tune you out, and who can blame him?

Finally, consciousness is just that: being awake and being there for your child. I am pained when I see babies' or very young children's cries ignored. Crying is the first language children speak. By turning our backs on them, we're saying,

'You don't matter.' Eventually, unattended babies stop crying altogether, and they also stop thriving. I've seen parents allow children to cry in the name of toughening them up ('I don't want him to get spoiled' or 'A little crying will do him good'). And I've seen mothers throw up their hands and say, 'Her sister needs me – she'll just have to wait.' But then she makes the baby wait, and wait and wait. There is no good reason for ignoring a child.

We are our children's best, and, for the first three years, only, teachers. We owe it to them to be P.C. parents – so that they can develop the best in themselves.

But Why Doesn't It Work?

'Why doesn't it work?' is by far one of the most common questions parents ask. Whether a mum is trying to get her seven-month-old to eat solid food, her two-year-old to use the potty or her toddler to stop hitting other kids, I often hear the old 'yes, but' response. 'Yes, I know you told me it will take time, but . . .' 'Yes, I know you said I have to take him out of the room when he begins to get aggressive, but . . .'

My baby whispering techniques do work. I've used them

myself with thousands of babies, and I've taught them to parents all over the globe. Granted, I know that some babies are more challenging than others – just like adults. Also, some periods of development, like when your child is teething or about to turn two, can be a bit hard on parents, as are unexpected illnesses (yours or your child's). But almost any problem can be solved by going back to the basics.

When problems persist, it's usually because of something the parents have done, or because of their attitude. So, if you're reading this book because you want to change a bad pattern and restore harmony to your family, and nothing seems to be working – not even my suggestions – really ask yourself if one of the following applies to you.

You're following your child, rather than establishing a routine. If you've read my first book, you know that I'm a firm believer in a structured routine (see Chapter 1). You start, ideally, from the day you bring your little bundle home from the hospital. Of course, if you didn't start then, you can also introduce a routine at eight weeks, or three months, or even later. But the older the baby, the more trouble you will have. And that's when I hear from parents, in a desperate phone call or an email like this:

I'm a first-time mother with Sofia, my 8½-week-old baby. I'm having problems setting a routine for her, as she is so inconsistent. What worries me is her erratic feeding and sleeping patterns. Please advise.

That's a classic case of following the baby. Little Sofia is not inconsistent – she's a baby. I'd bet the mother is inconsistent, because she's following her 8½-week-old daughter. This mum says she's trying to institute a routine, but she's really not taking charge. (I talk about what she should do in Chapter 1.) We're there to guide our children, not to follow them – and maintaining a routine is equally important with older babies and toddlers.

You've been doing accidental parenting. Unfortunately, in the heat of the moment, parents sometimes do anything to make their baby stop crying or to get a toddler to calm down. Often, the 'anything' turns into a bad habit that they later have to break – and that's accidental parenting.

You're not reading your child's cues. A mum will call me in desperation: 'He used to be on schedule, and now he's not. How do I get him back on track?' When I hear any version of that phrase – used to be and now is not – it not only means that the parents are letting the baby take over, it usually means they're paying more attention to the clock (or their own needs) than the baby himself. They're not reading his body language, tuning in to his cries.

You're not factoring in that young children change constantly. I also hear the 'used to be' phrase when parents don't realise that it's time to make a shift. A four-month-old who is on a routine designed for his first three months (see Chapter 1) will become cranky. The truth is that the only constant in the job of parenting is change.

You're looking for an easy fix. The older a child is, the harder it is to break a bad habit caused by accidental parenting, whether it's waking in the night and demanding a feed, or refusing to sit in a high chair for a proper meal. But many parents are looking for magic, expecting instant results. Remember the 'P' in P.C.: be patient.

You're not really committed to change. If you're trying to solve a problem, you have to want it solved – and have the determination and stamina to see it through to the end. Make a plan and stick with it. Don't go back to your old way and don't keep trying different techniques. If you stay with one solution, it will work . . . as long as you keep at it. Be persistent. I can't stress often enough: you have to be as consistent with the new way as you were with the old. Clearly, some children's temperament makes them more resistant to change than others (see Chapter 2), but almost all baulk when we change their routine. Stick with it and don't keep changing the rules and you child will get used to the new way.

Parents sometimes delude themselves. They will insist that they've been trying a particular technique for two weeks and say that it's not working. I know that can't be true, and, sure enough, when I really question them, I find out that, yes, they tried the technique for three or four days, and it worked, but a few days later they didn't follow through with the original plan. Exasperated, they tried something else instead. The poor child is then confused because they changed the rules on him; he's also often frightened.

If you're not going to see something through, don't do it. If you can't do it on your own, enlist backup people – your husband, your mother or mother-in-law, a good friend. Otherwise, you're more likely to give up on a technique, again confusing your child.

You're trying something that doesn't work for your family or your personality. When I suggest a structured routine or one of my strategies for breaking a bad pattern, I can usually tell whether it will work better for Mum or Dad – one's more of a disciplinarian, the other a softie. Some mothers (or fathers) will tip their hand by saying to me, 'I don't want her to cry.' The fact is, I'm not about forcing a baby to be or do anything, and I don't believe in allowing babies to cry it out. I don't believe in banishing toddlers to a solitary time-out, no matter how short the duration. Children need adults' help, and we have to be there to give it to them and, especially when you're trying to undo the effects of accidental parenting, it's hard work. If you're not comfortable doing a particular technique, either don't do it, or find ways to bolster yourself, by having the stronger parent take over for a bit, or enlisting someone to help.

It ain't broke – and you don't really need to fix it. I had an email from the parents of a four-month-old: 'My baby is sleeping through the night but he's only taking 725 ml (24 oz). In your book it says he should be taking 950–1075 ml (32–36 oz). How can I get the extra ounces in him?' How many mothers would give their right arm to have a baby sleeping through the night? Her child might have a smaller-than-average build. If his weight wasn't a concern to her paediatrician, my advice was to slow down and just observe her son; for now, nothing was wrong.

You have unrealistic expectations. Some parents are unrealistic about what it means to have a child. Often, they're very successful in their work: good leaders, smart and creative, and they view the transition to parenthood as another major life transition, which it clearly is. But it's also a very different passage because it brings with it a huge responsibility: caring for another human being. Babies and toddlers can't be managed with the same efficiency you apply to projects at work; they require care, constant vigilance and lots of loving time. Even if you have help, you need to know your child, and that takes time and energy. Keep in mind that, whatever stage your child is in right now – good or bad – will pass.

About This Book . . . and the Developmental Olympics

I'm not a big fan of age charts and never have been. Babies' challenges can't be sorted into neat piles. Of course, it's true that babies and toddlers generally reach certain milestones at designated times, but there's usually nothing wrong with those who don't. Still, in response to your request for greater clarity and specifics, here I have broken down my advice and tailored various techniques according to age groupings – birth to six weeks, six weeks to four months, four to six months, six to nine months, nine months to a year, one year to two, two years to three. My intention is to give you a better understanding of how your child thinks and sees the world.

If your child is already nearing his second birthday and you're considering potty training, you may wonder why I need to include information on his earlier development. Firstly, I hope that some of you may be reading this in advance as following my guidelines early on will help with potty training when you reach that milestone. But, if you haven't, don't fear. This early information about routine will help you understand my techniques for potty training and hopefully make it easier for all involved. I suggest you read that general information in Chapter 1 before going on to the potty-training technique specific to your child's age in the following chapters.

You'll notice that the age spans I cover are quite broad. That's to allow for variations among children. Furthermore, I don't want my readers to enter into what I call the 'developmental Olympics', comparing one child's progress or problems with another child's, or to become anxious if their little boy or girl doesn't fit a particular age profile. Too many times, I've witnessed playgroups composed of mothers who are observing each other's babies, comparing and wondering. First of all, in the life of a three-month-old, two weeks mean a lot – it's one-sixth of her life! Second, reading age charts in general raises parents' expectations. Third, children have different strengths and abilities. One might walk later than another, but she also might talk earlier.

I urge you to read all the stages, because earlier problems can persist – it's not uncommon to see a two-month-old concern crop up at five or six months. Besides, your child might be more advanced in a particular area, so it's a good idea to get a sense of what might lie ahead.

I also believe that there are 'prime times' – the best ages to teach a particular skill or to introduce a new element into your child's life. Particularly as children move into toddlerhood, if you don't start things at optimal times, you're likely to have a power struggle on your hands. You've got to plan ahead. If you haven't already made toddler tasks, such as dressing and toilet training, into a game or a pleasant experience, your child is more likely to baulk at the new experience.

Where We Go from Here

Throughout this book, I've tried to zero in on the most common concerns that parents have and then share with you the kinds of questions I typically ask to find out what's really going on (when I've reprinted emails and website postings, names and identifying details have been changed). I then suggest a different way of doing things, which will result in a different outcome from the one they've been getting. By letting you in on the way I think about babies' and toddlers' difficulties and how I come up with a plan, you can become the troubleshooter in your own family.

You can read this book cover to cover, or just look up the problems you're concerned about and go from there. However, I strongly recommend that you read through Chapter 1, which reviews my basic philosophy of child care. The following chapters then focus in depth on potty training as a specific area of concern.

You might be surprised by some of my suggestions and might not believe they'll work, but I have lots of examples to demonstrate how successfully they've been applied in other families. So why not at least try them with yours?

CHAPTER ONE

E.A.S.Y. Isn't Necessarily Easy (But It Works!)

Getting Your Baby on a Structured Routine

The Gift of E.A.S.Y.

You probably have a routine in the morning. You get up at roughly the same time, maybe you shower first or have your coffee, or perhaps you immediately hop on the treadmill or take your dog out for a brisk walk. Whatever you do, it's probably pretty much the same every morning. If by chance something interrupts that routine, it can throw off your whole day. And I'll bet there are other routines in your day as well. But let's say your routine's interrupted – your mealtime changes or you have to sleep in a bed away from home – isn't it unsettling and don't you feel disorientated when you wake?

Naturally, people vary in their need for structure. But even those who seem to spurn structure usually have some sort of dependable rituals during their day. Why? Because human beings, like most animals, thrive when they know how and when their needs are going to be met and what's coming next. We all like some degree of certainty in our lives.

Well, so do babies and young children. When a new mum brings her baby home from the hospital, I suggest a structured routine straightaway. I call it 'E.A.S.Y.', an acronym that stands for a predictable sequence of events that pretty much mirrors how adults live their lives, albeit in shorter chunks: **E**at, have some **A**ctivity and go to **S**leep, which leaves a bit of time for **Y**ou.

It is *not* a schedule, because you cannot fit a baby into a clock. It's a routine that gives the day structure and makes family life consistent. Everyone benefits: your baby knows what's coming next; siblings, if there are any, get more time with Mum and Dad; parents are less harried and have time for themselves as well.

The Birth of E.A.S.Y.

When I first started caring for newborns and young babies more than 20 years ago, a structured routine just seemed to make sense. Babies need us to show them the ropes – and to keep it up. The most effective learning comes with repetition.

I could also explain the importance of a structured routine to the parents I worked with, so that they could carry on after I'd left. I cautioned them to make sure that their baby always had some kind of activity after a feed instead of going right to sleep so that their little one wouldn't associate eating with sleeping.

The result? Because 'my' babies' lives were so predictable and calm, most of them were good eaters, they learned to play independently for increasingly longer periods, and they could get themselves to sleep without sucking on a bottle or breast or being rocked by their parents. As many of those babies grew into toddlers and preschoolers, I stayed in touch with their parents, who informed me that, not only were their children thriving in their daily routines, they were also confident in themselves and trusted that their parents would be there if they needed them. The parents themselves learned early on to tune into their child's cues by carefully observing their body language and listening to their cries and, because they could 'read' their child, they felt better equipped to deal with any bumps in the road.

'E.A.S.Y.' seemed a simple acronym designed to help parents remember the order of this structured routine. Eat, activity, sleep – it's the natural course of life – and then, as a bonus, time for you. With E.A.S.Y., you don't follow the baby; you take charge. You observe him carefully, tune in to his cues, but you take the lead, gently encouraging him to follow what you know will make him thrive.

E.A.S.Y. gives parents, especially first-timers, the confidence to know that they understand their baby, because they more quickly learn to distinguish their baby's cries. I've seen it time and again: parents who establish my E.A.S.Y. routine quickly get better at figuring out what their baby needs and wants at a particular time of day. Let's say you've fed your infant (the E), and she's been up for 15 minutes (the A – activity), and then she starts to get a bit fussy. Chances are, she's ready for sleep (the S). Conversely, if she's been napping for an hour (S), while you (the Y) hopefully have been stealing a little downtime for yourself, when she wakes, there's no guesswork involved. Even if she's not crying (though, if she's under six weeks, she probably is), it's a pretty safe bet that she's hungry. And so the E.A.S.Y. cycle begins again.

Write It Down!

Parents who actually chart their baby's day *by writing everything down* have less trouble sticking to a routine or establishing it for the first time. They are also better observers. Writing things down, even though it seems tedious (and, goodness knows, you have lots of other things to do!), will give you a much better perspective. You'll see patterns more readily, and see how sleep and eating and activity are interrelated. On days that your child feeds better, I'd just bet that he's less cranky during his awake time and sleeps better, too.

When E.A.S.Y. Seems Hard

In poring over the case files of thousands of babies I've worked with, as well as questions I have received from parents, I have tried to identify the stumbling blocks that typically occur when well-meaning and committed parents try to establish a structured routine.

It turns out that most parents' queries are not about routines. Instead, their questions tend to focus on a particular one of the letters of E.A.S.Y. They might ask, 'Why are my baby's feeds so short?' (the E), 'Why is he cranky and uninterested in his toys?' (the A), or 'Why does she wake up several times during the night?' (the S). But the three areas are interrelated: eating affects sleep and activity; activity affects eating and sleeping; sleep affects activity and eating – and all of them will naturally affect you.

Without a predictable routine, everything in a baby's life can go haywire – sometimes all at once. The solution is almost always E.A.S.Y.

Parents tell me, though, that E.A.S.Y. isn't necessarily easy. Here's a portion of a letter from Cathy, mother of one-month-old Carl and twenty-two-month-old Natalie. It captures the confusion and several of the difficulties parents seem to experience:

> My older daughter, Natalie, sleeps very well (seven to seven, puts herself to sleep, naps well). I can't remember how we got her there and need some sample routines to use as guidance for Carl, starting now and covering the next several months. He is breast-fed and I fear I inadvertently keep nursing him to sleep, and I sometimes confuse tired/hungry/wind pain. I need to have a general structure to follow to help me keep track of where I should be with him, since his sister demands a lot of attention when she is awake!

Cathy was ahead of the game in one respect. She at least realised that her problem was inconsistency and her inability to read Carl's cues. She suspected, quite accurately, that the solution is a routine. And, like many parents who have read about E.A.S.Y., all she needed was a bit of reassurance and further clarification. It didn't take her long to get on track as Carl was only a month old, young enough to adapt quickly to a new routine. As soon as Mum had her son on E.A.S.Y., she was better able to anticipate his needs.

All babies do thrive on routine, but some adapt more rapidly and readily than others because of their basic temperament (see Chapter 2). Cathy's first child, Natalie, who is now a toddler, was an extremely easygoing and adaptable infant. That would explain why Natalie napped and slept so well and also why Cathy can't remember how she got her there. But little Carl was a more sensitive type of child who, even at a month old, could be thrown off by a too-bright light or Mum holding his head slightly lower than usual when she fed him. Temperament affects how babies react to virtually everything in their lives.

With babies under four months old, problems also can occur because the parents don't realise that E.A.S.Y. has to be adapted to accommodate a special birth condition, like prematurity or jaundice (see pages 36, 39 and 40), or a particular infant's weight. Also, some parents misunderstand how to apply E.A.S.Y. For instance, they take 'every three hours' literally and wonder what kind of activity should be done in the middle of the night. (None – you send him right back to sleep.)

Parents also have problems with E.A.S.Y. when they think 'schedule' and focus more on reading the clock than reading their babies' signals. A *structured routine* is not the same thing as a schedule. If you try to fit a baby into a clock, then both mother and baby become frustrated. A schedule is about time slots whereas E.A.S.Y. is about keeping up the same daily pattern – eating, activity and sleeping – and repeating that pattern every day. The way humans learn – or other species, for that matter – is by doing something over and over, which is what a structured routine reinforces.

Parents often tend to live by schedules themselves so, when I write down a suggested three-hour routine for a baby who's under four months – say 7, 10, 1, 4, 7 and 10 – a schedule-driven mum sees the time slots as written in stone. She panics because one day her baby naps at 10.15 and the next day at 10.30. But you can't put a baby on a clock, especially in the first six weeks.

Sometimes you'll have a day when you're on track and everything goes smoothly and other days not. If you're busy watching the clock, instead of your baby, you'll miss important signals (like the first yawn in a six-week-old or eye-rubbing in a six-month-old, which means that your little one is getting sleepy). Then you have an overtired baby on your hands who can't get himself to sleep and who of course resists the routine, because it goes against his physical needs.

The most important aspect of E.A.S.Y. is to read your child's signs – of hunger, of fatigue, of overstimulation, of needing the toilet – which is more important than any time slot. So if, one day, he's hungry a little earlier, or seems tired before it's 'time' to put him down, don't let the clock threaten you. Let your common sense take over.

Guidelines to Get You Started

The E.A.S.Y. Log

When parents come home from the hospital and start E.A.S.Y., I usually suggest that they keep a log (there's one you can download from my website), so that they keep track of exactly what their baby is eating and doing, how long she's sleeping, and also what the mum is doing for herself.

Guidelines for Different Ages

Establishing a routine for the first time gets a bit harder as the baby grows, especially if you've never had structure. At least half of my queries come from parents who have either tried another, less-structured method, such as 'on-demand' feeding, or followed a different type of routine and found it lacking. Then they discover E.A.S.Y., and they wonder how to get started.

E.A.S.Y. is different with older babies, and my routine changes slightly with babies four months or older. Granted, babies' challenges don't necessarily fall into neat categories, but, as I explained in the Introduction, I have found that certain concerns seem to crop up in particular age groupings. Here, I will focus on:

- Birth to six weeks
- Six weeks to four months
- Four to six months
- Six to nine months
- Nine months and beyond

I will offer you an overall description of each stage, plus a list of the most common complaints and their probable causes.

No matter how old your child is, it's a good idea to read through all the sections because, as I will remind you repeatedly, you can't base strategies solely on age. Children, like grown-ups, are individuals. With a six-month-old baby, we sometimes see the same issues that crop up with a three-month-old baby, especially if the child has never had a routine.

The first six weeks: adjustment time

The first six weeks is the ideal time to start E.A.S.Y., which generally starts out as a three-hour plan. Your baby eats, plays after his feeds, you then set the scene for good napping. You rest while he rests, and, when he wakes up, the cycle starts again. But the first six weeks

How Babies Develop

Your baby will progress from being a totally dependent being to a little person who's more in control of his body. His routine will be affected by his growth and development, which happens from head to toe in this general order:

Birth to 3 months: From the head and shoulders up, including his mouth, enabling him to hold and lift his head and sit with support.

3 to 6 months: From the waist up, including the torso, shoulders, head, hands, enabling him to roll front to back, reach and grasp, and sit almost unaided.

6 months to a year: From the legs up, which includes the muscles and coordination that will enable him to sit unaided, roll back to front, stand upright, cruise, crawl and finally, at around a year or later, walk.

is also a time of huge adjustment, not just for your baby, but also for you, especially if you're a first-timer. And, if it's your second or third baby, you probably have his siblings underfoot, complaining about that crying blob who's suddenly monopolising everyone's time.

The baby doesn't have much control over anything at this point except his mouth, which he uses to suckle and to communicate. Crying is his voice, his only voice. The average baby cries somewhere between one and five hours out of 24. And, to most new parents, every minute feels like five.

We should never ignore a baby's cries or, in my opinion, let him cry it out! Instead, we always have to try to figure out what he's telling us. It's understandable, but, when the parents of young infants have problems with E.A.S.Y., it's usually because they're misreading their baby's cries, confusing a hungry cry with an overtired cry, for example.

Crying often peaks at six weeks, by which time observant parents have usually learned the language. Paying close attention to the baby's movement, they often act before the crying starts. But they also know what a hungry cry sounds like – a slight cough-like noise in the back of the throat, short to begin with and then as a more steady waa, waa, waa rhythm – compared to an overtired cry, which begins with three short wails, followed by a hard cry, then two short breaths and a longer, even louder cry. They also know their particular baby – after all, some are less vocal about their hunger than others. While some infants only fuss slightly and 'root' or curl the sides of their tongue, others become absolutely frantic with the first hunger pang.

If you put your baby on E.A.S.Y. straightaway, I guarantee you'll learn her cues more quickly and be better able to determine why she's crying. Looking at your daily chart will help. Let's say, for instance, that she fed at 7am. If she starts crying ten or fifteen minutes afterwards, and you can't calm her down, you can be fairly certain it's not hunger. More likely, it's a digestive issue and you'll know you have to do something that will calm her – not give her more food, which would only make her more uncomfortable.

The crying questions

When a six-week or younger baby cries, it's always easier to determine what she wants if you know where she is in her day. Ask yourself:

Is it time for a feed? (hunger)

Is her nappy wet or soiled? (discomfort or cold)

Has she been sitting in the same place or position without a change of scene? (boredom)

Has she been up for more than 30 minutes? (overtired)

Has she had lots of company or has there been a lot of activity in your household? (overstimulated)

Is she grimacing and pulling her legs up? (wind)

Is she crying inconsolably during or as much as an hour after feeds? (reflux)

Is she spitting up? (reflux)

Is her room too hot or cold, or is she under- or overdressed? (body temperature)

A Typical E.A.S.Y. Day for a 4-Week-Old		
E	7.00	Feed.
A	7.45	Nappy change; some playing and talking; watch cues for sleepiness.
S	8.15	Swaddle and lay your baby in the cot. It may take him 15–20 minutes to fall asleep for his 1st morning nap.
Y	8.30	You nap when he naps.
E	10.00	Feed.
A	10.45	See 7.45 above.
S	11.15	2nd morning nap.
Y	11.30	You nap or at least relax.

A Typical E.A.S.Y. Day for a 4-Week-Old (cont'd)

E	1.00	Feed.
A	1.45	See 7.45 above.
S	2.15	Afternoon nap.
Y	2.30	You nap or at least relax.
E	4.00	Feed.
A	4.45	See 7.45 above.
S	5.15	Catnap for 40–50 minutes to give him enough rest to handle his bath.
Y	5.30	Do something nice for yourself.
E	6.00	1st cluster feed (increasing your baby's intake in the early evening to help his sleep).
A	7.00	Bath, into night clothes, lullaby or other bedtime ritual.
S	7.30	Another catnap.
Y	7.30	You eat dinner.
E	8.00	2nd cluster feed.
A		None.
S		Put him right back to bed.
Y		Enjoy your short evening!
E	10-11	Dream feed (literally feeding your baby in his sleep; at the end of the dream feed, your baby will be so relaxed you can put him down without burping) and cross your fingers until morning!

Note: Whether a baby is breast- or bottle-fed, I advise the above routine – allowing for variations in times – until four months old. The 'A' time will be shorter for younger babies, and get progressively longer for older ones. I also recommend turning the two 'cluster feeds' into one (at around 5.30 or 6) by eight weeks. Continue the dream feed until seven months – unless he's a great sleeper and makes it through on his own.

Common complaints and probable causes

Complaint: I can't get my baby to conform to a three-hour routine. I can't get her to do even 20 minutes of activity time.

Cause: If your baby weighs less than 3 kg (6½ pounds) at birth, she may need to eat every two hours at first (see 'E.A.S.Y. by Weight' page 38). Don't try to keep her awake for activities.

Complaint: My baby often falls asleep during feeds and seems hungry an hour later.

Cause: This is common to premature, jaundiced, low birthweight and some simply sleepy babies. You might have to feed more often and definitely have to work at keeping him awake for his feeds. If breastfed, the cause could be improper latch-on, or mum's milk supply.

Complaint: My baby wants to eat every two hours.

Cause: If your baby weighs 3 kg (6½ pounds) or more, he may not be eating efficiently. Watch out that he doesn't turn into a 'snacker'. If breastfed, the cause could be improper latch-on, or mum's milk supply.

Complaint: My baby is rooting all the time and I keep thinking he's hungry, but he only takes a little bit at each feed.

Cause: Your baby may not be getting enough suckling time, so he's using the bottle or breast as a pacifier. He may be turning into a 'snacker'. Check your milk supply by doing a yield.

Complaint: My baby doesn't take regular naps.

Cause: He may be overstimulated by too much activity. Or you are not persevering with swaddling him and laying him down awake.

Complaint: My baby is a great napper, but she's up frequently at night.

Cause: Your baby has switched night for day and her daytime sleep is robbing her night-time sleep.

Complaint: I never know what my baby wants when he's crying.

Cause: Your baby may have a touchy or grumpy temperament (see Chapter 2) or have a physical problem, such as wind, reflux or colic. Whatever the cause, you and he will do better if he's on E.A.S.Y.

E.A.S.Y. by Weight

When the parent of a baby under six weeks has trouble with E.A.S.Y., I ask: **Did you have a full-term pregnancy?** Even if she says 'yes', I ask: **What was your baby's birthweight?** E.A.S.Y. was designed for an *average-weight* newborn – 3–3.5 kg (6½ to 8 pounds) – babies who generally can last three hours between feeds. If your baby weighs more or less, you will have to adjust accordingly (see the chart on page 42).

Babies who weigh more than average at birth – say 3.5–4.5 kg (8 to 10 pounds) – often feed a little more efficiently and take in more food at each feed. There's more weight on them, but you'd still keep them on the above three-hour routine. Age and weight are different things – a baby may weigh 3.5 kg (8 pounds) or more but, developmentally, he's still a newborn who needs to eat every three hours. I love to work with those babies, because I can get them to sleep longer stretches at night within the first two weeks.

However, some babies, because they're either premature or just smaller babies, weigh *less* at birth. They're not ready for the three-hour E.A.S.Y. plan. When parents bring them home from the hospital and try to put them on an E.A.S.Y. routine, the usual complaint is, 'I can't get her to do even 20 minutes of activity time' or 'She falls asleep during feeds.' They want to know how to keep her awake. Simple. You don't – at least not for activities. If you do, you'll overstimulate her, and she'll start to cry. As soon as you calm

Special Circumstances: Premature Births

Most hospitals put premature babies on a two-hour routine until they reach 2.25 kg (5 pounds). That's good news for parents, because it means that premature babies are already accustomed to the structure by the time they come home. But, because their tiny internal systems are so small and not quite developed, premature babies are also more prone to other problems, such as reflux and jaundice. Even more than low-birthweight babies, they tend to fall asleep on the job, so you have to be extra vigilant at waking them for their feeds. And you really have to protect their sleep by creating womb-like conditions: swaddle them and let them sleep in a quiet, warm, darkened room. Remember that they're not supposed to be here yet, and they want, and need, to sleep.

Special Circumstances: Jaundice

Just as birthweight changes how we introduce E.A.S.Y., so does jaundice, a condition in which the baby's bilirubin – the orange-yellow pigment of bile – doesn't get eliminated. Everything turns yellow – skin, eyes, palms of the hands and bottoms of the feet. The liver is like a car engine that hasn't quite cranked up, and it takes a few days to get it going. In the meantime, your baby will be very tired and want to sleep a lot. Don't be fooled into thinking you have a 'good sleeper' on your hands. Instead of letting her sleep, wake her every two hours, so that she gets the nourishment she needs to flush the jaundice out of her system.

The condition usually goes away in three or four days – slightly longer in breastfed babies than in formula-fed babies. You'll know everything's fine when her skin regains its pinkish hue and, lastly, the yellow disappears from the eyes.

her down, she'll probably be hungry again, because she's been crying, which uses up energy. And then you'll be utterly confused about her cries. Is she hungry? Tired? Windy?

At night, smaller babies can only last a maximum of four hours at first, so they generally have to feed at least twice a night in the first six weeks. But, if they go only three hours at a time, that's okay. They need the food. The fact is, you want little babies to eat and sleep a lot in the beginning, because you want them to get fat. If your baby is less than 3 kg (6½ pounds), put her on a two-hour eating schedule at first: feed for 30 or 40 minutes, reduce the activity time to only five or ten minutes, and then let her go to sleep for an hour and a half. When she's up, don't expect her to coo and goo at you – and keep stimulation to a minimum.

By being fed every two hours and getting the sleep time she needs to grow, she will definitely gain weight. As your baby starts to put on weight, she will probably last longer between feeds, and you'll be able to keep her up a little longer, gradually extending her activity time. Where she could only sustain 10 minutes up when she was first born, when she's 3 kg (6½ pounds), she can stay up for 20 minutes and by 7 pounds as long as 45 minutes. While she's putting on the weight, you'll gradually lengthen the two-hour routine, so that by 3–3.25 kg (6½ or 7 pounds), she'll be on the three-hour E.A.S.Y. plan.

E.A.S.Y. by Weight: The First Three Months

The chart overleaf shows how birthweight affects your baby's routine. (After four months, even most low-weight babies can last four hours between feeds.) You'll have to do the maths here. Note the time your baby usually wakes up, and write down approximate times based on your baby's weight and the information in the 'how often' column. Allow for variation – it's not the time slot that matters as much as predictability and order. To simplify, I've left out the 'Y' – time for You. If your baby weighs more than 3.5 kg (8 pounds), you'll be getting your night-times back a lot sooner than parents with smaller babies. If your baby weighs less than 3 kg (6½ pounds), you won't have much time for yourself, especially in the first six weeks. But hang in there – this phase will get better.

Weight	2.25–3 kg (5–6½ pounds)		3–3.5 kg (6½–8 pounds)		Over 3.5 kg (8 pounds)	
	How long	**How often**	**How long**	**How often**	**How long**	**How often**
Eat	30–40 minutes	Routine repeats every 2 hours during the day, until baby weighs 3 kg (6½ lb), at which point you can switch to an every-3-hour plan. At first these babies can only go 4 hours at night without eating.	25–40 minutes	Routine repeats every 2½–3 hours (for babies on the lower end of average) during the day; 4- to 5-hour stretches at night in the first 6 weeks, by which time you should be working at cutting out the 1 or 2am feed.	25–35 minutes	Routine repeats every 3 hours during the day. By 6 weeks, these babies can generally cut out the 1 or 2am feed and will do a 5- or 6-hour stretch from 11 to 4 or 5am.
Activity	5–10 minutes at first; 20 minutes at 3 kg (6½ lb), gradually extend time to 45 minutes when they are around 3.25 kg (7 lb).		20–45 minutes (includes nappy changing, dressing and, once a day, a bath).		20–45 minutes (includes nappy changing, dressing and, once a day, a bath).	
Sleep	1¼–1½ hours		1½–2 hours		1½–2 hours	

Six weeks to four months: unexpected wake-ups

Compared to the first six weeks at home – the classic postpartum period – during the next two and a half months or so, everyone starts to be on a more even keel. You're more confident, and, we hope, a little less harried. Your baby has put some weight on – even low-weight babies have often caught up by now – and is less likely to fall asleep during her feeds. Her feeds are still every three hours during the day, stretching a bit longer, though, as we get closer to the four-month mark. She is able to sustain longer activity periods, is probably sleeping for longer stretches at night, and her crying, which probably peaked at around six weeks, slowly starts to decline over the next two and a half months.

Common complaints and probable causes

Complaint: I can't get my baby to sleep more than three or four hours during the night.

Cause: She may not be getting enough food during the day, and you also might need to 'tank her up' before bedtime.

Complaint: My baby was sleeping for five or six hours during the night, but now she's waking up more frequently, but always at different times.

Cause: Your baby is probably having a growth spurt and needs more food during the day.

Complaint: I can't get my baby to nap for more than half an hour or 45 minutes.

Cause: You're probably either not getting him to bed when he first shows signs of fatigue, or you're going in too soon when he first stirs, which doesn't give him a chance to go back to sleep on his own.

Complaint: My baby wakes up at the same hour every night but never takes more than a few ml/oz when I try to feed him.

Cause: Habitual waking is almost never about hunger. Your baby is probably waking out of habit.

Have You Gone back to Work?

During the first three to six months, many mothers go back to a former job or begin to leave the house to work part-time. Some need to, some want to. Either way, change can cause glitches in the E.A.S.Y. routine.

Was your baby used to the routine before you went back to work? A good rule of thumb is never to make too many changes at once. If you know you're going back to work, institute E.A.S.Y. at least one month before you do. If you've already gone back, you might have to take two weeks off to get things on an even keel.

Who takes care of the baby in your absence? Does your carer understand the importance of a routine, and is he or she sticking to it? Is your baby's behaviour different at day care or with the carer in your own home than when he is with you? E.A.S.Y. doesn't work if people don't stick to it. You may not know whether your nanny or day care provider is following the routine you specify – except when your baby seems out of sorts when you pick her up. On the other hand, some parents, especially when the guilt kicks in, let the structure slip; that carer can often do a better job of keeping your baby on a routine.

How much is Dad involved? If you are trying to make changes in your baby's routine, how much are you prepared to allow him to be involved? I find that some mothers tell me they want a plan but don't actually carry it through, whereas their partner, perhaps the one who's home less, is better at sticking with it.

Have any other big changes happened in your household?
Babies are sentient beings. They tune in to their surroundings
in ways we don't yet understand. We know, for example, that
babies of depressed mothers tend to cry more themselves. So a
job change, a move, a new pet, illness in the family – anything
that disrupts the household equilibrium – can also disrupt your
baby's routine.

Four to six months: '4/4' and the beginnings of accidental parenting

At this stage, your baby's awareness is heightened and she
interacts more with the world around her than she did a few
months ago. She can hold up her head easily and is beginning
to grasp at things. She is learning to, or already can, roll over.
She can sit up fairly straight with your help, so her perspective
is changing, too. She's more aware of patterns and routine. She
has grown increasingly better at distinguishing where sounds
come from and figuring out cause and effect, so she's much
more engaged with toys that move and react to her touch. She
has a better memory, too.

Because of these strides in development, your baby's daily
routine naturally has to change, too – hence, my '4/4' rule of
thumb, which stands for 'four months/four-hour E.A.S.Y.'.

Most babies are ready at this point to switch from a three- to four-hour routine. It makes sense: your baby can play for increasingly longer periods during the day and sleep longer stretches at night. Whereas she used to wake up in the morning because she wanted a feed, most of the time now she wakes because of her own internal clock and not necessarily hunger.

Your baby is probably a more efficient eater, too, so draining a bottle or breast may take only around 20 to 30 minutes. Including a nappy change, then, the E is 45 minutes at most. But the A is different: now she can stay up a lot longer, typically another hour and a half at four months, two hours by six. Many kids have a two-hour nap in the morning but, even if your baby wakes up after one and a half hours, she can usually stay up the extra half hour while you're getting her ready for her next feed. Around 2 or 2.30, she'll want another nap, usually one and a half hours long.

Overleaf is a side-by-side glance to show how E.A.S.Y. changes when your baby is four months old. You can cut one feed because she's taking in more at each feed, consolidate three naps into two naps (keeping the late afternoon catnap in either case), and thereby extend your baby's waking hours.

Comparing the three-hour and four-hour routines

3-hour E.A.S.Y.	4-hour E.A.S.Y.
E: 7.00 Wake up and feed	E: 7.00 Wake up and feed
A: 7.30 or 7.45 (depending on how long feed takes)	A: 7.30
S: 8.30 (1½ hour nap)	S: 9.00 (1½–2 hour nap)
Y: Your choice	Y: Your choice
E: 10.00	E: 11.00
A: 10.30 or 10.45	A: 11.30
S: 11.30 (1½ hour nap)	S: 1.00 (1½–2 hours)
Y: Your choice	Y: Your choice
E: 1.00	E: 3.00
A: 1.30 or 1.45	A: 3.30
S: 2.30 (1½ hour nap)	S: 5.00 or 6.00 or somewhere in between: Catnap
Y: Your choice	Y: Your choice
E: 4.00 feed	E: 7.00 (cluster feed at 7.00 and 9.00, only if going through a growth spurt)
S: 5.00 or 6.00 or somewhere in between: Catnap (approximately 40 minutes) to get Baby through the next feed and bath	A: Bath
	S: 7.30 Bedtime
	Y: The evening is yours!

E: 7.00 (cluster feed at 7.00 and 9.00 if going through a growth spurt) A: Bath S: 7.30 Bedtime Y: The evening is yours! E: 10.00 or 11.00 Dream feed	E: 11.00 Dream feed (until 7 or 8 months, or whenever solid food is firmly established)

These are obviously ideal days. Your baby won't necessarily conform exactly to these times. Her routine can be affected by weight and temperamental differences, as some babies are better sleepers than others and some take less time to eat. Your child might even veer from her own schedule 15 minutes here and there. One day she'll have a shorter nap in the morning and a longer one in the afternoon, or she'll alternate between the two. The important consideration is that you stick to the eat/activity/sleep pattern (now at four-hour intervals).

Common complaints and probable causes

Complaint: My baby finishes her feeds so quickly, I'm afraid she's not getting enough to eat. It also throws off her routine.

Cause: The E may not be a problem at all – some babies are quite efficient eaters by now. You may be trying to keep your child on an E.A.S.Y. plan meant for a younger child – every three hours instead of every four.

Complaint: My baby never eats or sleeps at the same time.
Cause: Some variation in your daily routine is normal. But if he's snacking and catnapping – both the result of accidental parenting – he's never getting a good meal or a good sleep. He needs to be on a structured routine suitable for a four-month-old.

Complaint: My baby is still waking up frequently every night, and I never know whether or not to feed him.
Cause: If it's erratic waking, he's hungry and needs more food during the day; if it's habitual waking, you have accidentally reinforced a bad habit. You also might have him on a three- instead of four-hour routine.

Complaint: My baby makes it through the night but wakes up at five and wants to play.
Cause: You might be responding too early to his normal

early morning sounds and have inadvertently taught him that it's a good idea to wake up so early.

Complaint: I can't get my baby to nap for more than half an hour or 45 minutes – or she refuses to nap at all.
Cause: She may be overstimulated before naptime, or this is the result of a lack of, or improper, routine – or both.

In addition to the above, there are also continuing challenges that weren't dealt with earlier. Those seeds of accidental parenting planted earlier now begin to flower in the form of both eating and sleeping problems.

In some cases, it's because the parents didn't tailor E.A.S.Y. to their child's more advanced development. They didn't realise that they had to go from feeding every three hours to every four, that wake-up times are longer, or that naps are just as important as night-time sleep.

In others, it's because of the parents' inconsistency. They've gathered conflicting advice from books, friends, the internet or the TV and have been trying this strategy or that, constantly changing the rules on their baby, hoping that something will work.

Additionally, Mum may have returned to work full- or part-time, and that, or other types of household change, can disrupt a baby's routine. Whatever the circumstances, the problem is usually worse at this age because it has been going on longer.

Six to nine months: riding out the inconsistencies

The E.A.S.Y. plan is a different ball game now: although it's still a four-hour routine and there are many of the same problems I see in slightly younger babies, by six months there's a major growth spurt to contend with, too. It's the prime time to introduce solid food, and, by seven months or so, to cut out the dream feed.

Mealtimes are a little longer – and a lot messier – as your baby gets to try a whole new way of eating. In the beginning, babies are like eating machines, but, at around eight months, your baby's metabolism starts to change. She often becomes leaner, losing her baby fat, which has been put on to give her the strength to move around. At this stage it's more important to gauge her diet by quality not quantity.

Now, too, the early evening catnap disappears, and most babies are down to two naps a day – ideally, each one lasting one to two hours. Napping is not a favourite pastime of babies at this stage. As one mum put it, 'I think it is because Seth is aware of the world now, and can move around more so he doesn't want to sleep. He wants to see everything!' True enough, as physical development now takes centre stage. Your baby can hold himself upright – by eight months he'll be able to sit on his own – and he is becoming more coordinated as well. He'll be a lot more independent, especially if you've nurtured this skill by allowing him to play on his own.

The common complaints at this stage are pretty much the same as we saw at four to six months – except, of course, habits are more deeply entrenched and a bit harder to change. Eating issues and sleep disturbances that could be tweaked in a few days at earlier stages now can be very intractable. They are never impossible to correct, but will take a little longer to solve.

Otherwise, the biggest issue that crops up at this point is inconsistency. Some days your baby will take a long nap in the morning, other days it happens in the afternoon, and still other days it seems he's decided to drop one of his naps altogether. One day she'll eat with gusto, and the next she'd rather skip meals. Some mums roll with these ups and downs, and others want to tear their hair out. The key to survival is twofold: if he doesn't stick to a routine, at least you can.

As the mother of a seven-month-old (who'd had her baby on E.A.S.Y. from the time she brought him home from the hospital) remarked, 'The one thing I have learned is that practically every baby who is on this routine is different – you really do just have to do what suits you both.'

The fact is, because babies nine months and older can stay up for longer stretches without sleeping, it is possible for them to start skipping the morning nap altogether and take one long nap in the afternoon – for as long as three hours. They eat, play, eat again, play some more and then go to sleep. In other words, 'E.A.S.Y.' becomes 'E.A.E.A.S.Y.'

I also get a lot of queries on my website from parents of babies this age who have tried E.A.S.Y. or another type of routine when their child was younger. This is the age that they decide to try again. Here is a typical posting:

> When my baby was two months, I tried to put her on E.A.S.Y., but the sleep part was so difficult, and the nursing was so often I gave up. Now that she is older I would like to try it again, but I would like to see sample schedules of other babies too.

E.A.S.Y. after nine months

Sometime between nine months and a year, your baby will be able to go five hours between feeds. He'll be eating three meals a day, just like everyone else in the family, and have two snacks to tide him over. He can be on the go for two and a half to three hours, and, usually around 18 months – earlier in some children, later in others – get by on one big nap in the afternoon. We're not technically following E.A.S.Y. at this point, more likely he's on E.A.E.A.S.Y., but it's still a structured routine – and it should continue to help you with everything, from potty training to general behavioural issues. Every day may not be exactly the same, but the elements of predictability and repetition are still there.

Starting E.A.S.Y. at Four Months or Older

If your baby is four months or older, and she's never had a routine, it's time to put her on one. It will take patience, but it will be worth it in the end. The process is different from that of younger babies for three important reasons:

1. *It's a four-hour routine.* Sometimes parents don't realise they have to adjust the routine to their child's more advanced development. Their baby is eating more efficiently and sustaining ever-increasing periods of activity but they're still feeding her every three hours – in effect, they're trying

to turn back the clock. While they reason, quite correctly, that their child is having a growth spurt, they need to feed her more at each feed, rather than more often.

2. *We use my 'pick-up/put-down method' (P.U./P.D.) to make changes.* With babies over four months old, sleep difficulties are invariably part of the reason why it's impossible to sustain a daily routine, if not the entire problem. This is when I introduce beleaguered and sceptical parents to P.U./P.D., a technique I rarely advise for younger babies (for a detailed description of this key sleep strategy, see either *The Baby Whisperer Solves All Your Problems* or *Top Tips from the Baby Whisperer: Sleep*).

3. *Establishing a structured routine over four months is almost always complicated by accidental parenting.* Because parents have already tried other methods, or a medley of methods, their baby is confused. And, in most cases, the baby has already got into a bad habit, such as falling asleep on the breast or waking repeatedly during the night. Therefore, putting an older baby on E.A.S.Y. invariably involves more commitment and work, a bit of sacrifice, and a great deal of consistency.

The older the baby, obviously, the harder it will be to change his routine, especially if he's still waking at night and is not used to any type of structure in his day. Bear in mind that it took at least four months for those bad habits to develop. It won't take nearly that long to get rid of them if you stick with the plan.

Because babies are individuals, and because what happens inside each of their homes is different, too, I need to find out exactly what the parents have been doing so that I can tailor my strategies accordingly. If you've read thus far, you should already be anticipating the kinds of questions I'd ask parents whose baby has never had a routine:

E: How often are you feeding your baby? How long are his feeds? How many ml/oz of formula or breast milk is he eating during the day? If he's close to the six-month mark, have you also introduced solid food? Although it's only a guideline, see how your baby measures up on the E.A.S.Y. by Weight chart (see page 42). If he's eating every three hours or less, that's inappropriate for a four-months or older child. If his feeds are too short, he might be a snacker; if too long, he may be using you as a pacifier. Also, babies who aren't on a routine by four months often eat too little during the day and get up at night for additional feeds. Particularly if they're over six months, they often need more sustenance than a liquid diet provides.

A: Is he more alert than ever? Is he starting to roll over? What kinds of activities does your child do during the day – play on a mat, attend a Mother and Baby group, sit in front of the TV? It's sometimes harder to establish a schedule with a more active baby, especially if he's never had one. You also have to make sure that you're not doing too much with your baby, which would make it hard for him to calm down for naps and bedtime and disrupt his eating as well.

S: Is he sleeping through at least six hours in the night – which he should be by four months – or does he still wake for a feed? What time does he get up in the morning, and do you go right in to him or allow him to play independently in his cot? Does he nap well, and for how long? Do you put him in his cot for naps, or do you just allow him to get exhausted and sleep wherever he passes out? The S questions help gauge whether you've been allowing your baby to learn how to self-soothe and get to sleep on his own, whether you've taken charge of his sleeping, or let him lead you. The latter, obviously, leads to problems.

Y: Have you been under more stress than usual? Have you been ill? Depressed? Do you have support from your partner, your family, your friends? It takes stamina and dedication to establish a routine if your life has been chaotic. If you're not up to speed, make sure that you nurture your adult needs first. It's almost impossible to minister to a baby, if it feels like *you* need to be taken care of. If you don't have support, get some. Having someone else by your side to give you a break is great, but even a shoulder to cry on is better than nothing.

The thing to keep in mind when introducing a routine for the first time is that there are rarely overnight miracles – three days, a week, even two, but never overnight. When ushering in any new regime to a baby or child of any age, you're going to get resistance. You may say you want your baby on the E.A.S.Y. routine but, to do so, you have to take certain actions. Especially if your baby hasn't ever had a routine, you may have to forfeit something for a few weeks – your own time. Many parents resist that notion, like the mum who assured me she'd 'do anything' to get her baby on E.A.S.Y., all the while firing off a barrage of questions: 'Do I have to stay home every day in order to get him on a routine? Or can I go out with him and have him take naps in the car seat? If I have to stay home, will I ever get out of the house with my son? Please help me.'

Have some perspective. Once your baby gets used to the E.A.S.Y. routine, you don't have to feel like a prisoner. Fit your errands into your baby's time. You might feed the baby and then his A time will be riding in the car with you and doing errands. Or you might do a feed and activity at home, and let your baby sleep in the car seat or pram. (Your baby may not nap as long, though, if he's the type who wakes up when the car engine turns off.)

However, when you're first trying to establish a routine, the ideal would be for you and your partner to stay at home for a fortnight to give your child a chance to get used to a new routine, a week at the least. You must make the time to make the change. During this critical introductory phase, see to it that his feeds, his activities, and his sleep times happen in a familiar environment. Just two weeks, mind you, not the rest of your life. Yes, the first few days will be especially tough because you've already programmed this baby in a different way and now you have to undo the old patterns. But, if you hang in there, E.A.S.Y. will work.

When you try to change things, your baby is going to say (with his cries), 'What the hell are you doing? We don't do it this way! I'm screaming as loud as I can, but you're not listening!' The good news is that babies' memories are relatively small. After a few really tough days or weeks, you'll find that it is better – no more erratic feeds, no waking up in the middle of the night, no frustrating days when you don't understand what he wants. If you're as consistent with the new way as you have been with the old, he'll eventually get used to it.

Chapter Two

E.E.A.S.Y. Does It

When Should We Start?

Potty Panic

Although parents of babies and young children worry most about sleep issues (with eating running a close second), their anxiety seems to reach new heights when they even think about toilet training. When do you start? How do you start? What if my child is resistant? What if she has accidents? The questions are endless.

Although parents sometimes fret over the various other physical milestones if they occur later than the books predict (or later than their child's playmates exhibit), they nevertheless take each one in their stride, allowing time for mind and muscles to kick in. And yet, those same parents will become very agitated about their child learning to eliminate in the toilet, which is really just another milestone.

The statistics show that, in the last 60 years, the age of

training children has been significantly postponed – in part because of the trend towards child-centred child-rearing, and in part because disposable nappies do such a good job that children don't feel uncomfortable when they're wet or soiled. The results of this delay are dramatic. Where, until recently, children were potty trained at about 18 months, now the *average* age for potty training children is between the age of three and four, with some children as old as seven still wearing disposable nappies.

Maybe the later training gives parents more time to worry about what might go wrong, or perhaps their anxiety is one that even parents who trained their kids early felt: bathroom habits have underlying 'moral' implications. In any case, it's clear that modern parents have trouble viewing the transition from nappies to toilet seat with the same detachment they allow for sitting or walking, or even talking.

I say, 'Relax.' Teaching your child how to go to the bathroom is really no different from any of the developmental milestones you've managed to get through thus far. And, if you view it purely as another milestone, your attitude might change.

Think of it this way: you don't expect your child to get up on her feet one day and be ready to run a marathon. You know that development doesn't just happen – it is a process, not an event. For each milestone, there are signs and steps along the way. For example, long before your child actually takes a step, you watch joyfully as she tries to pull herself up. You realise she's practising and that soon her legs will become strong enough to support her. Then she starts cruising, holding on to the furniture (or your leg). This is her first experience in propelling her little legs forwards. One day, you notice that she is starting to experiment with letting go of her supports. First, she lifts one hand and then two. She looks at you and you respond with a big smile and verbal praise.

She keeps practising and eventually she is strong and confident enough to take a first step. Seeing this, you hold out your arms to encourage her, or perhaps you give her your hand to steady her as she takes a few more steps. A week or two later, she refuses to hold your hand altogether, non-verbally letting you know, 'I can do it myself.'

If she tries to make a turn or lift a toy, she ends up on her rear, but, as the months go on, she becomes a totally upright human who can not only walk but can also carry things and jump and even run. When you look back, you realise that she 'started to walk' four to six months earlier.

Developmentally, the same thing happens with elimination.

The signs that your child is ready to relieve herself into a toilet instead of her nappy start long before she actually goes on the toilet. But we often don't pay attention to the signs, and we don't encourage the independence.

Part of the problem is that the baby isn't uncomfortable – modern disposable nappies do their job so well that she barely feels wet. Add to that the fact that most of us lead such hectic lives, it feels overwhelming and time consuming to make a commitment to toilet training. 'It can wait' is the typical attitude nowadays, and it's reinforced by the experts who tell us that our children need to 'mature' before we can even attempt to train them. The problem is, we wait too long.

Starting at Nine Months Can Be E.E.A.S.Y.

Although a small contingent of experts take an extreme position on toilet training (see the box on the Toilet-training Continuum opposite), the conventional wisdom (from both books and paediatricians) about toilet training is that children *can't* be taught to eliminate in the toilet before the age of two and that some won't achieve success until well into their third year. While it is generally acknowledged that some babies will achieve toilet readiness earlier, just as some have different temperaments (see page 74) or are 'early' or 'late' walkers or talkers, most experts nevertheless advise parents to wait until their child exhibits most, if not all, of the signs of readiness. The belief is that the child has to comprehend what the training is all about and that the child's sphincter muscles have to be fully mature (which begins at around a year).

Though I originally subscribed to the traditional theory of toilet training children at 18 months, after working with scores of parents, reading the current research on toilet training and observing what happens in the rest of the world, I find myself disagreeing with both the conventional wisdom and the extremists.

That is not to say that I don't find positive points at either end of the toilet-training continuum. The child-

The Toilet-training Continuum

Just about every subject in parenting finds advocates on either extreme. As always, both sides make some good points.

Child-centred Training. A theory that took root in the early 1960s, this end of the continuum believes toilet training should be solely up to the child. Parents show by example, look for the signs, and give the child opportunities to use the toilet, but never push. The idea is that, when a child is ready, he'll ask to use the toilet. It might not happen until your child is four.

Nappyless Babies. Advocated by those who observe that, in America prior to the 1950s, babies were toilet trained much earlier and that, in primitive cultures, babies go without nappies

The Toilet-training Continuum *cont'd*

from birth, the goal is to teach the child to tune in to his elimination needs and sensations – even before he's old enough to sit. When parents read the baby's cues and body language, they hold him over a toilet (or bucket) and make a cuing sound, like 'ssss' or say 'pee-pee'. Thus, the child is conditioned to eliminate with an adult's assistance.

My own theory comes somewhat in the middle of these two ends of the continuum.

centred approach honours a child's feelings – a basic precept of baby whispering. However, allowing a child to decide when he's 'ready' and for him to guide himself through toilet training is like giving him a bowl of food on the floor and expecting him to develop table manners. He might, but what are parents for if not to guide their children and socialise them?

Moreover, if the child is *starting* the process at two or two and a half, that's already 'late' in my eyes, because, by then, children are less interested in pleasing their parents and more determined to do things their way; the parents easily lose control of the process.

As for the nappyless school – also called 'elimination communication' – I can't fault a method that relies heavily on observing the child and giving him cues. I also believe that it's good to give a child opportunities to practise new skills before he is actually able to master them.

And I certainly agree that training should start earlier than is usually done – particularly in the United States. According to advocates of nappyless training, 80 per cent of children in the rest of the world are toilet trained between 12 and 18 months, while, in the USA, the average age of completion is between 36 and 48 months.

However, I have trouble with any model that creates a philosophy based purely on primitive culture. We're living in a modern society. I don't think it's advisable to hold an infant over a bucket or even a toilet seat. Equally importantly, I believe the child should have some control, some input, and some understanding of the process. Putting him on a toilet before he can sit up on his own is, in my opinion, too early.

Not surprisingly, therefore, I come down somewhere in the middle of the two extremes, because I recommend starting toilet training at around nine months, or whenever your baby is able to sit steadily and comfortably on his own. Many of the babies whose parents have followed my plan achieve complete daytime control by their first birthday. Some don't, of course, but research shows that even they are usually trained by the time their peers are just starting out.

Why Nine Months?

Many of you are sceptical, if not shocked, when I suggest starting toilet training as early as nine months. So allow me to explain. At nine months, I view the process of elimination as part of a baby's daily routine – a parent's job is to make him conscious of it.

Just as there's time for eating, activity and sleep, you also make time for elimination. Twenty minutes after your baby eats or drinks, you put him on the toilet. In effect, you've got him on an 'E.E.A.S.Y.' routine – eat, elimination, activity, sleep, and time for you (which admittedly becomes less and less as your child approaches toddlerhood). The two Es in E.E.A.S.Y. are switched when your child gets up in the morning, because then you'll put him on the toilet straightaway, before he eats (see 'The Plan' on pages 98–102).

When you start training between nine months and a year, naturally, your baby doesn't have the control or consciousness of an older child. Hence, toilet training is less about teaching your baby as much as about conditioning him.

By putting him on the toilet seat at times that he normally goes to the bathroom, or when he exhibits signs that he's about to pee or poo (which is usually after he's eaten), you're likely to catch him, perhaps not every time but sometimes. He feels the toilet seat, and he learns to release his sphincter muscles. When he does, you cheer him on, just as you did when he started pulling himself upright. He's at an age where he still wants to please you (which he most assuredly won't want to do at around the age of two), and that positive reinforcement will help him realise that the accidental act of elimination is something you value.

By starting early, you're also giving him practice in allowing his sphincter muscles to relax and to release his pee and poo into a receptacle rather than his nappy. And isn't that what acquiring a skill is all about? Practice, practice, practice!

In contrast, when you wait until he's two, he's already got accustomed to eliminating into a nappy, and he then has to learn not only to tune in to his own body signals but also to be willing to release his waste elsewhere. He's also had no practice.

It would be like expecting a child to walk but keeping him in his cot in a sitting position until you thought it was 'time' for him to do so. Without those months of trial and error, strengthening his legs, and learning how to coordinate his movements, he wouldn't be very good on his feet, would he?

The Signs that Your Child is Ready

Because the current conventional wisdom about toilet training is so widespread – powered in part by the disposable nappy industry that profits from late toilet training – many parents simply ignore their own observations and knowledge of their child.

For example, this posting, from the mother of a 15-month-old girl, appeared on my website:

> For the last two months we have been sitting Jessica on the potty before bath time, because she kept wanting to sit on the big toilet. Most of the time nothing happens, but every now and again she pees. Yay! Just luck and timing, I'm sure!
>
> But here's the weird thing. Last week, she started to randomly bring me new nappies during the day, flattening them out on the floor and lying on top of them. At first I thought it was just funny and dismissed it without another thought, but I could not get Jessie away from it, so finally I decided I might as well just humour her and move on. Sure enough, she had a poo bum!
>
> This has gone on for six days now and, if I ask her, 'Do you have a poo bum?' she says 'yes', and she is always right. Also, she has never brought me a nappy when she is dry and clean.
>
> Is this a sign of potty-training readiness – so soon? In a way, that would be great because I am home with her until September. On

the other hand, I don't want to push her into something she's not ready for. Any thoughts?

Sadly, Jessica's mother has all the signs right there in front of her but, because of what most books, articles and internet sites advise about toilet training, she's not paying enough attention to *her* child.

The so-called gospel ('Don't start before 18 months') is reinforced by other mothers. One mum wrote in response, 'Yes, I'd say it's a sign but, if it's the only one, I wouldn't really start potty training. She's telling you after the fact and not before. Plus, it's only for poo and not for pee, which is more often. But I'd say she's getting the idea and so hopefully she will figure it out *before* she goes.'

Figure it out? Jessica is only 15 months. Would her mother also leave her to 'figure out' how to use a spoon, dress herself or behave with other children? I would hope not.

Toilet training is not an overnight event. It is a process that starts with a child's awareness, which Jessica clearly has. She is telling her mother after the fact, because no one is helping her connect the physical sensations. She needs explanations and examples. Finally, it's absolute poppycock to believe that a child needs to show *all* the signs of readiness in order to initiate training.

Toilet-training Checklist

You will undoubtedly find hundreds of similar checklists in other books and on the internet. I am including this (from the American Academy of Pediatrics), but I urge you to view all checklists with caution.

Some benchmarks are reached later than others. Observant parents will notice facial expressions and postures that signal that their child is peeing or pooing *long* before he learns to walk or undress himself and way before he actually asks for grown-up underwear. Also, children mature at different rates and have different levels of tolerance for being soiled.

Use your common sense and your knowledge of your child. It is *not* necessary for him to have reached *all* of these in order for you to begin toilet training:

✓ Your child stays dry at least two hours at a time during the day or is dry after naps.

Your Child's Temperament

As with any developmental step in a child's life, children with different temperaments will react in different ways and be ready at different times. If you are aware of your child's temperament, you will find it easier to tailor their potty training specifically to them.

Nature and nurture

Every baby's emotional makeup is predetermined, at least in part, by his biology – genes and brain chemistry. You can look at your own family tree to see how temperament is passed on from one generation to the next like some kind of emotional virus. Haven't you found yourself saying that your baby is 'as mellow as I am' or that your mother has said, 'Davy is as grumpy as Aunt Sue'? Clearly, baby temperament is inborn – that's their *nature*. But, by studying identical twins, who have exactly the same genes but rarely the same personalities by the time they reach adulthood, scientists have concluded that environment – *nurture* – is equally influential.

Babies are different *at birth*. Some are sensitive and cry more than others, some are barely affected by what's going on around them. Some seem to greet the world with open arms; some cast a suspicious eye on their environment.

Some practitioners and researchers cite three or four types of infant, while others say there are as many as nine. I believe there are five broad temperamental types: *Angel*, *Textbook*, *Touchy*, *Spirited* and *Grumpy*. But the bottom line is one on which most observers agree: temperament – which is sometimes referred to as 'personality', 'nature' or 'disposition' – is the raw material that babies possess when they come into the world. Temperament (and,

> ## Toilet-training Checklist *cont'd*
>
> ✓ Bowel movements become regular and predictable.
> ✓ Facial expressions, posture or words reveal that your child is about to urinate or have a bowel movement.
> ✓ Your child can follow simple instructions.
> ✓ Your child can walk to and from the bathroom and can help to undress himself.
> ✓ Your child seems uncomfortable with soiled nappies and wants to be changed.
> ✓ Your child asks to use the toilet or potty chair.
> ✓ Your child asks to wear grown-up underwear.

admittedly, some types are easier to handle than others) affects how they eat, sleep and react to the world around them, including how you go about potty training them.

In order to work *with* your baby's temperament, you have to really understand it. Rifling through my mental filing cabinet, I've come up with five children, who exemplify each type, and given them pseudonyms that begin with the same first letter: Alicia (*Angel*), Trevor (*Textbook*), Tara (*Touchy*), Samuel (*Spirited*) and Gabriella (*Grumpy*). Keep in mind that the following thumbnail descriptions highlight *dominant* qualities and behaviour. You may recognise your child in a particular category or you may feel she's a cross between two of them.

Temperamental Types

Angel. Alicia, now four, is just what her label implies: a dream child, one who easily adapts to her environment and to whatever changes you throw her way. As a baby, she rarely cried and, when she did, it was never hard to read her cues. Her mum hardly remembers her terrible twos – in short, she is rarely hard to deal with because her predominant emotional style is easygoing and even-tempered. It's not that she never gets upset, but, when she does, it doesn't take much to distract or calm her. As a baby she was never rattled by loud noises or bright lights. She has always been very portable, too – her mum could go from store to store without worrying about a meltdown. From the time she was a wee infant, Alicia was a good sleeper. At bedtime, you simply laid her in her cot and she'd happily drift off with her dummy, needing almost no other encouragement. In the morning, she babbled to her stuffed animals until someone came in. She adapted easily to a big-girl bed when she was 18 months. Even as a baby, she was a social being, smiling at whoever came her way. To this day, she fits in easily when confronted with new situations, play groups or other social settings. Even when her baby brother came along last year, Alicia took the change in her stride. She loves being Mum's little helper.

How Angel babies are often described: 'Good as gold.' 'Didn't even know I had a baby in the house.' 'I could have five children like him.' 'We were really lucky.'

Textbook. Seven-month-old Trevor has reached every milestone like clockwork. He had a growth spurt at six weeks, slept through the night by three months, rolled over by five, sat up at seven, and I'll just bet that when he's a year old, he'll be walking. Because he's so predictable, his mother has no trouble reading his cues. For the most part, he has a mellow temperament, but he also has his cranky periods – just like the books describe. However, it's a relatively simple matter to calm and reassure him. As long as his mother introduces new things slowly and gradually – a good rule of thumb with any baby – Trevor goes with the flow. All his firsts thus far, like his first bath or his first taste of solid food, have been pretty uneventful. It takes Trevor 20 minutes to fall asleep for a nap or night-time sleep – the 'average' time for a baby – and, if he's restless, he responds well to an extra pat and a reassuring 'shush-shush' in his ear. From the time he was eight weeks old, Trevor could amuse himself with his own fingers or a simple toy, and every month since then he has become a little more independent, playing on his own for increasingly longer periods. Because he's only seven months, he doesn't yet 'play' with other babies, but he's not frightened to be around them. He's fairly good in new places – his mum has already taken him on a trip abroad to see his grandparents. When he got home, it took him a few days to reorientate himself, but that's normal for any baby who travels through different time zones.

HOW TEXTBOOK BABIES ARE OFTEN DESCRIBED: 'She's right on time with everything.' 'She's mellow unless she needs something.' 'A low-maintenance child.'

Touchy. Tara, now two, had a slightly below-average birthweight, and was also ultrasensitive from the beginning. By three months old, she had put on weight, but emotionally she was highly strung and easily excitable. She flinched at noises, blinked and turned her head away in bright light. She cried often and for no apparent reason. During her first few months, her parents had to swaddle her and make sure that her room was warm enough and dark enough for her to sleep. The slightest noises disturbed her and it was hard for her to get back to sleep. Everything new to Tara has to be introduced extremely slowly and very gradually. (Studies have indicated that the internal systems of babies like Tara are in fact different from other children's. Because they possess more of the stress hormones cortisol and norepinephrine, which activate the fight-or-flight mechanism, they actually *experience* fear and other feelings more intensely.) Shy of strangers as a baby, Tara would tuck her head into Mum's shoulder. As a toddler, she is bashful, fearful and cautious. She tends to clutch her mother in any new situation. At play group, she's getting a little more comfortable with the children, a carefully selected group of mellow kids, but it's still hard for her mum to leave the room. With help, Tara comes out of her shell, but it takes lots of time and patience on her parents' part. Tara is great at puzzles and games that require concentration, a trait that will probably carry over once she starts school. Touchy children often become quite good students, perhaps because they find the solitary work more manageable than running about with their classmates in the school playground.

How Touchy babies are often described: 'A real crybaby.' 'The slightest thing sets him off.' 'He's not good with other people.' 'He always ends up in my lap or clinging to my leg.'

Spirited. Four-year-old Samuel is a fraternal twin, the 'wilder one'. A sonogram prior to delivery showed his brother in the lower position, but Sam somehow managed to squeeze his way past Alexander to emerge first. He's been doing that ever since. He is aggressive and very vocal. As a baby and toddler, his loud screams always let his parents know, 'I need you . . . now!' In social situations, such as family gatherings or play groups, he jumps right into the middle of the action. Sam always wants whatever toy his brother, or another child, is playing with. He loves stimulation and is drawn to anything that bangs, pops or flashes. He's never been a good sleeper and, even at four, has to be coaxed into bed at night. He eats well, and is a sturdy chap, but he can't sit at a table for very long. Sam climbs incessantly and heedlessly. Not surprisingly, he often gets into dangerous situations. He sometimes bites or pushes other children. And he throws fits when his parents don't give him what he wants, or don't do it fast enough.

If Spirited children sound like they're challenging, they are. But, properly handled, they are also born leaders. They can become captains of sports teams in secondary school and, as adults, explorers and entrepreneurs who are fearless about plunging ahead where others have dared not go. The hard part is getting them to channel that wonderful energy.

HOW SPIRITED BABIES ARE OFTEN DESCRIBED: 'A handful.' 'Always into something.' 'I don't have the energy to keep up with her.' 'She's fearless.'

Grumpy. Gabriella seems like she's got a chip on her shoulder, and she's only three. As a baby, it was hard to make her smile. Dressing, and changing her nappies, has always been a challenge. She tended, even as a baby, to go stiff on the changing table and then become fidgety and irritable. In her early months, she hated being swaddled and would cry for a long time whenever her parents tried. Luckily her parents got her on to a routine as soon as she came home from the hospital, but whenever they veered slightly from it, Gabriella loudly voiced her displeasure. Feeding has been difficult all along, too. She was a breastfed baby, but getting her to latch on and stay with it took a lot of work on Mum's part. Gabriella was also slow to adapt to solid food and even today is not a great eater. She gets impatient if food isn't presented the moment she's ready for it and exactly the way she likes it. She's a quirky eater, preferring certain foods over others and sticking with them no matter how much her parents coax her. She is social when she wants to be, but she tends to hold back to assess each new situation. In truth, she prefers to play on her own and tends to resent other children being in her space. But Gabriella is also a character; she has a mind of her own and isn't afraid to use it.

Grumpy children teach their parents patience. They're also good at maintaining their own boundaries. You simply can't push them, a trait that later on makes them persevere with problems. As children and adults they tend to be very independent and good at taking care of and amusing themselves.

How Grumpy babies are often described: 'What a sourpuss.' 'He seems to prefer playing on his own.' 'I feel like I'm always waiting for his next meltdown.' 'He always has to have his way.'

Nurture: How Parents Override Temperament

Temperament is not a life sentence. Although Nature provides what babies come in with, children's experience – the nurture they get, starting in infancy – has just as much of an impact. In other words, your baby's emotional life is determined both by her temperament, which shows itself as early as a few days after birth, and her life history – events, experiences and, most importantly, the people who care for her. Parents can have a beneficial effect on children's temperament, or just the opposite, because their young brains are still mouldable. I've seen Touchy babies grow out of their shyness to become poised, sociable teenagers. I've watched Grumpy children grow up and find a special niche for themselves. And I know lots of Spirited kids who go on to be responsible leaders instead of troublemakers. But the reverse is true, too. Any type of child, no matter how good her innate disposition, is at risk if parents don't heed her needs and wants. An Angel can become a grouch, a Textbook toddler can turn into a terror. The key is to work with your child's nature.

Even before Katha was born, her mum, Lillian, knew that she had a very active and assertive little girl on her hands. In utero, Katha kicked incessantly, as if to send a message: 'Here I am and you'd better get ready.' Once in the world, Katha did not disappoint. She was a typical Spirited baby who demanded her mum's breast and cried immediately if it took too long for the milk to start flowing. Seemingly more interested in being awake than sleeping – she might miss something – Katha resisted going to bed and usually managed to get out of her swaddle. Fortunately, Lil put Katha on a good routine from day one. As her little spitfire grew into toddlerhood, she made sure that Katha, who walked at nine months, had ample opportunity to put her energy to good use in the morning and they spent lots of time outdoors. In the afternoon, they did quiet activities because Lil knew how hard it was for Katha to wind down. It was particularly challenging when Katha's little sister arrived on the scene. Not surprisingly, Katha did not like to share Mum's attention. But Lillian made special 'big girl' places for Katha in the house ('where the baby isn't allowed') and made sure that she spent one-on-one time with her energetic older daughter. Today, at five, Katha is still a bold and adventurous child but also polite and fairly well behaved because her parents have reined her in and limited her behaviour when she was unable to control herself. Katha is also a precocious athlete – the result no doubt of all the climbing and ball playing her mum encouraged. Lillian had no illusions that her firstborn would grow out of her temperament; instead, she worked with her nature.

Look at the Child You *Have*

Children like Katha are innately more of a challenge than others, but all children do better with 'P.C.' parents like Lillian who understand and accept their child's nature and who tailor their day and, when needed, discipline accordingly. But parents are not always able to, and in some cases don't want to, see what's right in front of them.

Almost every pregnant couple have preconceived notions of who that child will be and what he or she will be capable of doing. Usually our fantasies reflect who we are. So the athlete imagines herself out on the football field or hitting tennis balls with her child. The hard-driving lawyer thinks about how smart his kid is going to be, where he's going to go to school, and what great discussions the two of them will have. Very often, however, our real children don't come close to the ones parents see in their daydreams. They might have imagined an angelic child but when reality hits there's a squirming, screaming little devil, interrupting dinner, waking them up at night.

As your baby gets older and certain emotional traits become more apparent – grumpiness, sensitivity, feistiness – it's also bound to remind you of yourself or your partner or your Great Aunt Tillie. So let's say you have a Spirited baby. If you are a go-getter and feel positive about high-energy people, you might boast: 'My Charlie is as assertive as I am.' But, if you're somewhat overwhelmed by, or fearful of, the Spirited child's set of traits, you're likely to have just the opposite response: 'Oh, I hope Charlie doesn't turn out to be as aggressive as his dad. I'm afraid he'll turn into a bully.' Of course, we're bound to see family traits re-emerge in our children, but, remember, *he is a different person, with different influences, and a path all his own.* And most important, if you teach your Spirited child how to manage his emotions and to channel his energy, he doesn't have to become a bully.

The trouble with fears or fantasies is that when we act on them and not on what we see in front of us, the real-life child suffers. So one of the first orders of baby whispering is: **Look at the child you have, rather than at the fantasy of the one you *wanted* to have.**

Grace, a very shy woman herself, called me because she was concerned about Mack's 'stranger anxiety'. On the phone she explained that her seven-month-old was turning out to be 'just like me' at that age. When I met seven-month-old Mack, I saw a Textbook baby who was a little skittish about new people and, given a few moments to adjust, to Grace's surprise, he was happily sitting on my lap.

After asking Grace to look at her own behaviour honestly, the truth came out: Grace never *allowed* Mack to get close to anyone else. She hovered over her son constantly, keeping everyone away because she believed she was the only one who understood how painful it was to be so sensitive. In her mind, she was the only one who could protect him and knew how to handle him. Even worse, Grace did what many worried parents do: she voiced her concerns in Mack's presence.

Oh, but you say, Mack was just a *baby*. But babies learn from listening and watching. Researchers aren't sure exactly when understanding really kicks in but we do know babies pick up on their caretakers' feelings and we do know that they understand long before they start to talk. So when Mack hears, 'He never goes to anyone else,' it tells him that no one else is safe.

Parents' Temperament

Parents' understanding of their children's emotional life is often thwarted when their baby's temperament clashes with their own emotional style. The fact is, *every* parent has a temperamental style all their own. They were a baby once themselves and fitted into one of the five categories I described earlier, or perhaps they were a blend of two or more. An array of experiences have influenced them since then, but their temperament – their emotional style – is still a factor in how they relate to people and situations.

Healthy development is not just about your baby's temperament; it's also about your demands and expectations – whether you see your baby for who she really is and can adapt your strategies to fit her needs, not just yours. My experience with thousands of parents has given me a pretty good idea of what happens when a parent with a particular emotional style interacts with each of the baby types.

Confident parents are easygoing and calm, so they're a good fit with all of the baby types. When they first have a child, they tend to roll with the changes in their life and with the ups and downs of parenthood. They're fairly carefree about the job – 'naturals' who trust their intuition and are very good at reading their baby's cues. Because they're usually pretty laid-back and patient, they do well with Grumpy babies, are willing to take the extra time that Touchy babies need, and have the stamina and creativity to raise Spirited kids. Confident parents tend to think the best of everyone, and so they look for the best in their child. Though they have their own opinion about various parenting practices, they're very open to new ideas, and they're quick to recognise when they're attributing their own motives to something their baby is doing.

By-the-book parents sometimes open themselves up to a lot of frustration, because they expect their baby not to deviate from the norm. When problems arise, these are parents who search wildly in books and magazines and on the internet to find their exact situation and a recipe for correcting it. They try to get their baby to conform to what's typical – not necessarily because it's good for the baby but because it's 'normal'. The ideal baby for these parents is a Textbook baby who reaches milestones right on time. They do well with Angel babies, too, because they're such adaptable children. But, because By-the-book parents want so desperately to keep to a schedule, they may miss the baby's signs. So it's not a great fit for a Touchy baby who is ultrasensitive, or a Spirited baby who is anything but a conformist. By-the-book parents run themselves round in circles, trying various schedules and strategies, depending on which book or expert they're following today. Probably the worst fit is with a Grumpy baby, who will get even more upset with each new change. By-the-book parents' strength lies in their ability to research and deal with problems. They are extremely open to suggestions.

Highly strung parents are sensitive themselves. They may be shy, so it's hard for them to reach out to other parents for company and support. Highly strung mums often get weepy and feel incompetent in the early days of motherhood; highly strung dads are afraid to hold the baby. With an Angel or Textbook baby, they are usually okay although, if the baby is having a bad day, as all babies sometimes do, they think they must have done something to cause it. They have a low tolerance for noise and are very bothered by crying, so a Touchy or Grumpy baby is rarely a good fit. They're likely to feel frustrated and weepy much of the time. If they have a Grumpy baby, they're likely to take her moods personally. Highly strung parents tend to be overwhelmed most of all by a Spirited baby, who quickly learns that he's in charge. Their sensitivity has a positive side as well: they are extremely tuned in.

Go-getter parents are always on the move, always involved in a project. Go-getter parents can't sit still; they may have trouble with the fact that a baby slows them down and may even have quick tempers. Go-getter parents tend to resist advice. Though many call me to ask what to do, if I give them a plan, they're likely to come back with a series of 'Yes, but . . .' statements and 'What if . . .?' questions. As they tend to schlepp their baby everywhere, Go-getter parents could even wear out an even-tempered Angel or a Textbook baby or, worse, make them insecure in all the chaos. In the process, they often miss what's in front of them: the joy in having a child most other parents would be grateful for. Go-getter parents might get angry at a Touchy baby, feel affronted by a Grumpy baby's bad humour or lack of adaptability, and lock horns with a Spirited baby. They tend to be somewhat rigid and to favour extreme approaches. They don't do well with E.A.S.Y. because, when they hear 'routine', they think *schedule*. On the other hand, these are very creative parents who expose their children to a wide variety of experiences and encourage them to try new things and take risks.

Headstrong parents seem to think they know it all and get upset when their baby doesn't respond as they think she should. They're very opinionated and often stubborn, and it can be hard for them to compromise. These parents are always moaning and complaining. Even if they have an Angel or Textbook baby, they find and focus on the one thing their baby doesn't do or, in their minds, is doing wrong. Headstrong parents find it hard to tolerate a Touchy baby's crying. They don't like the bother of having to calm down or chase after a Spirited baby constantly. And they resent that their Grumpy baby is so stubborn and doesn't smile very much, perhaps because it reminds them of their own nature. In short, these parents find a way to criticise and carp no matter what kind of baby they have. To make matters worse, they complain about their babies to others when the children are within earshot and, in doing so, these parents turn their little ones into what they keep telling them they are. The good thing about Headstrong parents is that they have a lot of staying power. Once they recognise a problem, they're open to suggestion, and are willing to follow through, even when the going gets hard.

Be aware of your and your child's temperament

The above emotional styles are composites taken to the extreme. No one fits any category exactly; most of us see pieces of ourselves in each one. But, if we're honest, we know who we are most of the time. Also, I'm not implying that parents aren't allowed to make mistakes. Parents are only human. Their needs are always simmering beneath the surface, and they have lives and interests outside their children (and that's a good thing).

My purpose in showing you the possible 'poorness of fit' scenarios is that this will heighten your awareness and make you a bit more conscious about how your style might affect your child's emotional fitness. If parents are able to see through the veil of their own self-interest and bring their demands and expectations into line with their child's temperament and abilities, that child's emotional fitness will bloom and everything, from weaning to playing and, yes, even to potty training, will be easier.

How Long Will it Take?

So when will your child be totally nappy-free? There's no way of my predicting that. It will depend on when you start, your commitment and patience, your child's body, your child's (and your) personality, and whatever else is going on in your household.

I can tell you, however, that, if you observe your child carefully, stick with the plan (see pages 98–102), and treat toilet training as you would any other developmental milestone, it will be a far easier transition for your child than if you panic.

CHAPTER THREE
Getting Started

Nine to Fifteen Months

If you initiate toilet training between nine and 15 months as I suggest, you might see some of the typical signs of readiness (see Checklist on pages 74–75), but you also might not. That's okay. If your child is old enough to sit independently, she's ready to start. View the process as an interesting challenge rather than a daunting task. You're her guide.

What you'll need. I prefer the seats that you put on top of the regular toilet to a free-standing potty, because that's one less transition you'll have to make. In this age range, there's rarely resistance to the toilet, because children are so eager to please and to participate. Make sure that the seat has a little foot rest – it will make your child feel safe and also comes in handy if she needs to push out a bowel movement.

Most nine- to 15-month-olds don't yet have the coordination to climb up and down without an adult's help, but it's important to invest in a sturdy little step stool, too, because you'll want to encourage her independence. She can use it to get on and off the toilet and also to reach the sink for other bathroom rituals, like teeth-brushing and hand-washing.

Get yourself a notebook to record your child's toilet habits (see the Checklist).

Don't start this process when you're extremely busy with a project, about to move, about to take a holiday or when either of you is ill. You'll need patience – plan to stick with it for the long haul.

How to prepare. Toilet training at a young age (and older for that matter) starts with careful observation of your baby and her daily routine. If you've embraced my philosophy of care (see Chapter 1) and have tuned in to your child, you know her cries and body language, and have responded to the little person she is. By the time she is nine months old you will have no problem discerning how she acts right before she's about to pee or poo. When she was only a few months old, for example, she probably stopped sucking whenever she had a bowel movement – babies can't focus on more than two things at once.

Keep your eye out now for signs – also see the box for common signs. Your baby might also have signals of her own but, I guarantee, if you keep your eyes open, you'll figure out what your child does when she's about to eliminate.

Take notes. Context and routine can also be a guide. By nine months old, many babies have bowel movements at pretty much the same time every day. They often urinate 20 to 30 minutes after taking in liquid. This knowledge, coupled with your observation, should give you a pretty good sense of when and how often during the day your child relieves herself.

> ## Common Signs of a Bowel Movement
>
> **If she's not walking yet:**
>
> She might get a funny expression on her face
>
> She might grunt or grimace
>
> She might just stop what she's doing in order to concentrate on the process
>
> **If she's started walking:**
>
> She might go into a corner or behind a couch when she poos
>
> She might grab her nappy, try to peek inside it, or reach in to feel what's come out of her

Even if you don't think she understands you, comment on her bodily functions in whatever way you talk about these things in your family: 'Are you pooing, honey?'

Just as important, comment on your own habits: 'Mummy has to go to the bathroom.' Ideally, you're not too shy to actually show your child how you do it. It's always a good idea to have the same-sex parent demonstrate, but that's not always possible. Since little boys initially learn to pee while sitting down (and that's how their dads should first show them), seeing Mummy sitting on the toilet is a good example, too. Children learn by imitation, and they desperately want to do what their parents do. You're starting to make your baby more conscious of what's happening in her body when she has to pee or poo. It's hard to put the sensations into words, especially because you might feel a full bladder in a different way from your child. She has to learn by experience.

The plan. For the first few weeks, place your child on the toilet as soon as she wakes up. Make it part of her morning ritual. You walk into her room, greet her with a big kiss, throw open the curtains, lift her out of the cot and say, 'Time to go to the toilet.' Do not ask. Just do it. The way brushing her teeth becomes part of her bedtime ritual, going to the bathroom – and hand-washing afterwards – should become part of her morning wake-up.

Of course, she will have peed during the night, and her nappy will be wet. She may or may not pee again. Leave her on the toilet only a few minutes – never more than five. Squat down or sit on a stool, so you're at eye-level. Read a book, sing a song, talk about the day ahead. If she urinates, identify it ('Oh, look, you're peeing like Mummy does, and it's going into the toilet') and praise it (the only occasion I suggest that parents go utterly overboard with praise). But be sure to comment on the act itself. In other words, don't say, 'What a good girl,' rather 'What a good job.'

Also, show her how to wipe herself. At this age, it's better for you to do the wiping, especially after a poo, but explain it and let your child try it on her own.

> ### Elimination Control
>
> Typically, children gain control over their sphincter muscles in this order:
>
> 1. night-time bowel control
> 2. daytime bowel control
> 3. daytime bladder control
> 4. night-time bladder control

With little girls, remember to teach them to wipe front to back.

If she doesn't pee, just take her off the toilet, put on a new nappy, and give her breakfast.

If you have a son, he might have an erection. I don't like those penis guards on some of the child-size toilet liners and potties because little boys' parts can get caught on them. They also don't teach the child to hold his penis down and aim into the bowl. At first, you'll have to do it for him. A good way is to tuck his penis between his legs and gently hold his little thighs together.

Twenty minutes after your child has a drink, put him on the toilet again and repeat the process. You should do this for the rest of the day as well, after meals and at times when you think he usually has a bowel movement.

Also, children often pee and/or poo right before a bath, or they do it in the tub. If that's on your child's agenda, put him on the toilet before his bath as well. Always use the same words. 'Let's go to the toilet. Let's get your nappy off. Here, I'll help you up.' These are all cue words that will help him associate the bodily functions with the toilet.

If you build these little visits into the normal routine of your day – E.E.A.S.Y. – just as you go to the bathroom several times a day, the process will seem quite natural to him. You can also include hand-washing as part of the ritual.

Go slowly for the first few weeks, but be consistent. You might find some people suggest putting children on the toilet only once a day at first, but I think that's confusing. Why do we use the toilet just at breakfast or just before a bath? The idea is to put your child in touch with his body and to help him make the connection between elimination and sitting on the toilet. Your baby may not have complete control over his sphincter muscles (see Elimination Control box on page 99) until he's a year or older, but even an immature sphincter muscle sends out a signal that he will recognise. By placing him on the toilet, you're providing him with an opportunity to recognise the sensation and practise control.

Remember that your child is not going to be trained in a week or two. But he will quickly begin to make the association and, before you know it, he'll think the whole thing is so much fun he'll want to go to the toilet even when you don't suggest it. For example, Shelley, who recently started this plan with one-year-old Tyrone, called after a few weeks, exasperated. 'He constantly wants to sit on the toilet, and most of the time he doesn't go. To be honest, Tracy, I'm fed up. I don't act angry of course, but it's a waste of time when Tyrone just sits there.'

I told Shelley that she had to keep it up, no matter how frustrating – or boring – it was. 'It's trial and error at first, but you're helping him recognise the physical sensations of his body. You can't quit now.' Shelley's experience is very common. After all, the toilet is a very exciting experience for a young toddler: it has water in it and a handle that makes the water swirl around. Actually doing something while you're sitting there is far less important to your child than to you. But he will eventually do it, and you will act like he's won the lottery when he's successful. The joy of sharing his accomplishment is really all a baby needs to drive him to succeed. The more supportive you are, the better the results.

When to Lose the Nappy

As soon as he has been dry for a week during the day – without any accidents – you should switch him to underwear. I don't like using disposable pull-ups because they're too much like disposable nappies, which don't allow a child to *feel* wet.

It usually takes a few weeks or months longer for children to get through the night. Assume that it's safe to leave a nappy off at night when he's woken up dry for two weeks.

CHAPTER FOUR
Potty Training an Older Child

Sixteen to Twenty-three Months, and Beyond

Let's say you've read my suggestions about toilet training, but are still sceptical. Nine months, or even a year, in your opinion, is just too young.

Marla, for one, protested when I suggested that she start 11-month-old Harry straightaway, because he was saying 'pee-pee' a lot and also seemed to hate being in a soiled nappy. 'But he's such a baby, Tracy,' she insisted. 'How can I do that to him?' She was determined to wait until Harry was at least 18 months, or two, or even older. That's her choice – and it might be yours.

You might also look back and realise starting earlier would have been a great idea, but your child is already two. That's fine, as long as you know that the plan will be slightly different and that waiting until a child is two years or older means you

Naked Training?

Lots of books and experts suggest initiating toilet training in the summer so that you can let your child go naked or at least bottomless. I don't agree. To me, that's like stripping a child down at each meal so he doesn't get food on himself. I think we need to teach children how to behave civilly in the real world. The only time I believe in naked toilet-going is right before the bath.

will have all the other toddler behaviours to deal with on top of toilet training.

Still Cooperative: Sixteen to Twenty-three Months

This is my second-favourite time to initiate toilet training because, at this age, a child still wants to please his parents. You'll proceed much in the same way as you would with a younger child, but the communication will be easier, because your child understands everything now. His bladder is also bigger, so he won't pee quite as often, and he now has more control over his sphincter muscles. The trick is to make him aware of how and when to exert that control.

What you'll need. A child-size toilet seat. Even though your child is not going to spend more than five minutes at a time on the toilet seat, it's a good idea to get a few books that are read only in the bathroom: some about toilet training itself, others that your child just enjoys.

Take your child shopping and let him pick out his new big-kid underpants. Stress that they're like the kind that Mummy or Daddy wear. Buy at least eight pairs because there will be accidents.

How to prepare. In the same way as if you were starting earlier, if you don't already know what your child looks like before he's about to poo or pee, start paying attention. In older children, the signals are usually more pronounced. Take note of your child's pre-elimination behaviour; write it down.

In the month preceding training, change his nappy more often, so that he gets to feel what 'dry' is – and begins to prefer it to wet. Children this age usually urinate 40 minutes after drinking. During the week before you initiate toilet training, change your child every 40 minutes, or at least check his nappy for wetness, so that you can get a good idea of his patterns.

Use this time to discuss toilet training, making sure that you use the language of elimination, so as to heighten your child's awareness of the process ('Ooh, I see you're pooing'). If he tugs on his nappy, say, 'You're wet. Let me change you.'

It's especially important to model bathroom skills ('Want to come into the bathroom and watch Dad pee?'), and read books and/or watch videos about going to the toilet.

Whether your child is in cloth or disposable nappies, I also suggest showing your child where poo really belongs by taking him into the bathroom and letting him see you flush the poo down the toilet.

Some experts suggest placing an inanimate object on a toilet as a way of demonstrating. But, although it works with some children and there's no harm in it, I think putting a doll, an action figure, or a teddy bear on the toilet makes no sense whatsoever, and many young children won't be able to make the symbolic leap. Young children learn by human example, role modelling and demonstration. They want to do what Mum and Dad do. Doesn't it make sense that, for them to learn how to go to the bathroom, you *show* them how it is done?

The plan. As described for earlier training, put him on the toilet the moment he wakes up.

When you get him dressed, put him into underpants or heavy cotton training pants, *not a nappy and not disposable pull-ups.* It's important for him to feel a different sensation on his bottom, and to feel wet if he has an accident.

Put him on the toilet half an hour after meals or after a snack and a drink. Never ask, 'Do you want to go to the toilet?' unless you want to hear 'No' for an answer. Factor in the reality that, at this age, children take their play very seriously. When you make these trips to the bathroom, instead of interrupting your child just as he's about to complete a major task such as stacking a brick on top of another, wait until he's done.

Sit with him, but never longer than five minutes. Distract him from the process by reading a book or singing a song. Don't pressure him (but you can run the water to bring on a tinkle!)

Success will be an accident at first but, once your child starts making the connection, it becomes a reinforcing cycle, especially if you go overboard on the praise.

Your child is now quite capable of expressing his likes and dislikes, and, particularly if you're starting this process close to the age of two, you might get some resistance. If your child is resistant, he might not be ready. Wait two weeks and try again.

If he has an accident, don't make a big deal of it. Just say, 'It's okay. Next time you can do it.' Remember to empty bowel movements into the toilet to show where it goes ('This time I'll put it in the toilet for you').

Trainer Cups and Toilet Training

Many parents nowadays encourage their children to walk around with a beverage in hand. With the advent of non-spillable trainer cups it's easier than constantly asking, 'Are you thirsty?' As long as you use water or water with a splash of juice, there's no harm in this practice *except* when toilet training. What goes in must come out! You might want to limit drinks to regular times – after meals, two hours between meals as a snack – so that the liquids at least come out at predictable times.

Before the age of two, most children don't think of themselves as 'smelly' or 'messy', so eliminate such words from your banter. Only an adult's negative response teaches a child that there's something to be ashamed of.

Avoiding Power Struggles: Two to Three and Beyond

Even though the preparation and plan will be basically the same after the age of two as before, parents often get into power struggles over toilet training because their child is much more independent and capable, and not necessarily interested in pleasing her parents. Your child now has a very distinct personality, likes and dislikes.

Some children have a low tolerance for wearing a wet or dirty nappy and will actually ask to be changed. Obviously, they will be easier to train. If your child is generally cooperative and responsive to directions, that bodes well for toilet training, too.

If you are consistent, even at this age, your child will learn to use the toilet. Keep E.E.A.S.Y. in mind and weave bathroom visits into the fabric of your daily routine: 'We just had lunch, and you had something to drink, so we go to the toilet, and wash our hands.' You can also explain more at this age: once the child is aware of his own pee and poo signals, you can say, 'You just have to hold it in long enough to sit down on the toilet and let go.'

What if it Becomes a Power Struggle?

Often parents will ask me, 'How do you know whether a child is being resistant or just isn't ready?' This email is typical:

> My two-year-old puts up a battle every time I want to take her to the toilet. Some friends have told me that she's just not ready, but I also think she's just being a toddler. Should I give it up? If so, when should I try again?

Most children are ready by age two, although resistance goes with the territory, so it can be a dicey time to start. But it's not an insurmountable problem. One of the biggest mistakes I see parents make is that they stop and start and stop and start. This is unadvisable at any age, but particularly at two and beyond. Your child really understands what is happening now, and toilet training can become a great way to manipulate you.

Don't engage in battles over toilet training. However, if your child is resistant, *stop only for a day, two at most.* You'd be surprised; a day does matter. Besides, your child is a lot older now and, if you wait a week or two, he's already a lot older and might be even more resistant.

Keep trying. Don't force the issue, but don't give in altogether.

Make the experience pleasant, using distraction and rewards. Some parents create a toilet chart and dole out gold stars for each successful trip to the bathroom. Others bribe with sweets or chocolate that isn't allowed at any other time. I'm all for rewards, but you also know your child and what works best – some kids couldn't care less about them; others thrive with incentive systems. If your child doesn't deposit anything into the toilet, don't praise or reward the effort. Try again in half an hour. If he wets in the meantime, don't make a big deal out of it. Just make sure that you have clean underwear and clothing at the ready.

A two-year-old is quite capable of changing his own clothes. If he's wet, it's simply a matter of putting on new bottoms. If he's soiled, have him step into the bathtub fully clothed and tell him to take off his own clothes and wash himself. This isn't a form of punishment – rather, it's a way of him really feeling the consequences. You're there to assist, but you must put him in charge of the clean-up. Don't lecture or humiliate him in the process. Just make him a partner and show him that he needs to share the responsibility.

For your own information, try to figure out whether it really was an accident, or whether your child was purposely waiting until he got off the toilet to relieve himself. If the latter, you know that he's figured out a way to use the toilet as blackmail and that he's looking for attention. The best strategy would be to give him positive attention in other ways – spend more one-on-one time and give him a special job to do with you, like sorting socks when you fold the laundry. Give him a little section of your garden to plant, or a pot for the windowsill. As he watches it grow, draw the parallel: 'It's growing up, just like you are.'

Watch your own temperament and reactions as well. Especially if you've been at it for a while, you're going to be more emotional about this process, and your child will sense your tension. It's a sure formula for a battle.

At this age, be prepared for all the age-appropriate acts of rebellion – kicking, biting, screaming, back arching and other types of tantrum behaviour.

Introduce the elements of choice (ensuring they're around the toilet experience, not whether your child wants to go to the toilet): 'Do you want me to go first, or do you want to go on the toilet before me?' or 'Would you like me to read this book to you, or would you like to look at it yourself while you sit here?'

What About Night-time Training?

At this age, although children do have accidents at night, once you see continued dryness during the day, and dry nappies on waking, he's likely to have success at night, too. (Interestingly, very few of the queries I get from parents of toddlers focus on night-time problems, which tells me that, once you get the daytime elimination routine going, night dryness follows quite naturally.)

Use the same rule of thumb for night-time training as daytime when it comes to getting rid of nappies. When your child has woken up dry for two weeks, switch to underpants, or just let him wear his pyjama bottoms.

Obviously, limit the water and other liquids he consumes before bedtime.

CHAPTER FIVE

Toilet Troubles

Troubleshooting the Most Common Problems

With your real-life problems – from my website, inbox and client files – in each case, the first two questions I ask are: **When did you start toilet training?** and **Have you been consistent?** I've found that toilet troubles are caused, at least in part, by parents' lack of follow-through. They start (in my opinion, too late) and then, at the first sign of resistance, stop and start again, often more than once; before they know it, they're into a battle of wills. You'll see that theme in many of the following cases:

'Shows No Readiness at Twenty-two Months'

My almost 22-month-old son, Carson, started saying 'pee-pee' last week. I asked him did he have to go pee-pee or has he already done pee-pee? I didn't really get a response one way or the other. He has not shown any readiness for toilet learning. He could be in a nappy ready to explode from urine and not care. We have a potty in the bathroom for him and right now he uses it to stand on to get at the sink. I don't know if he is saying pee-pee just because it is a new word he knows or if he has figured out what it means. Should I try putting him on the potty when he says pee-pee? He has seen both me and my husband in the bathroom plenty of times and I tell him, 'We are going potty.' I'm trying to lay some groundwork. Also, when do you start putting your child in pull-ups? He is still in ordinary nappies. I don't think I need to bother with pull-ups until he is ready for toilet learning.

At his age, Carson understands everything. He might be one of those boys who couldn't care less about sitting in pee and poo, but he is certainly capable of knowing that pee and poo belong in the toilet, especially if he's been observing his parents. I also don't agree that he 'hasn't shown any readiness'. He very likely knows what 'pee-pee' is and what it means.

I'd ask, **Have you tried putting him on the toilet at all?** I suspect not. Well, what is Mum waiting for? She has to start a plan and stick to it, putting her son on the toilet 40 minutes after he drinks. Also, give him a crate or a little step stool for reaching the sink. Otherwise, how will he understand the true purpose of a toilet? Better yet, get him a small seat to put over the regular toilet. He already knows that's what Mum and

Dad use, and then you won't have to make another transition later on.

I would remind this mother that toilet training takes lots of patience. She needs to leave less to chance, and take a more active role in getting her son trained.

'Two-and-a-Half-Year-Old Not Trained after a Year of Trying'

Betsy is 2½ years old. We've been working on toilet training since she was about 18 months old. She's wearing pull-ups now. Some days she refuses to use the toilet at all and screams her objections to it. Yesterday, she sat through dinner with a soaking wet pull-up on and didn't even tell us. When the mood strikes her she'll use the toilet. When we're out she'll ask to use the bathroom but usually it's for something to do. How can I get her toilet trained?

When I hear a case like this, where a child started training at 18 months and a year later is using the toilet only when 'the mood strikes her', especially if it's a girl (they do generally learn faster than boys), I know that the parents have been inconsistent – and, I have to add, lazy.

Part of the problem is that disposable nappies let parents off the hook by removing the guilt that would be felt about leaving a child in a wet nappy. Hence, we live in a culture in which many parents don't feel motivated to start toilet training in the first place, and then they switch to pull-ups, which aren't much better.

With Betsy, I'd tell Mum to take her shopping for some big-girl underwear immediately. Betsy might be a lot less complacent about sitting through a meal in soggy cotton underpants as opposed to pull-ups. If she wets or soils them, she has to change herself.

But I think there's more to this story, too. Because Betsy 'screams' when she doesn't want to go to the toilet, I'd ask her mother, **Do you ask if she wants to go to the toilet or simply tell her it's time to go?** With a child this age, it's always more effective to tell her, 'It's time to go to the toilet,' and give her an incentive, 'and when we come back we can play teatime together.'

I sense here, too, that Mum is frustrated with the process (who wouldn't be after a year?)

Does your child have tantrums around other requests that you make? Perhaps Betsy is temperamentally strong willed. If her mother isn't handling her tantrums well in other contexts, she's certainly not going to have success in the bathroom. At two and a half, the child is in control of the elimination process, not the parent. **Have you ever lost your temper or reprimanded your child for soiling herself?** If so, Mum has to take a deep breath and do something about her own behaviour. Threats aren't good teaching tools. I would suggest then that Mum take herself out of the equation as much as possible. Instead of her reminding Betsy about the toilet, she could set a timer and explain to Betsy that when the bell rings, it's time to sit on the toilet.

Finally, with a child like Betsy, incentive programmes work well. To design an effective one, I'd ask Betsy's mum, **What motivates your child?** Some children love to get stars that eventually add up to a special outing. Others perform for the sake of an after-dinner mint.

'Tried Everything – and Still Not Trained at Three and a Half'

My son, Louis, is 3½. I have tried everything I can think of, but he refuses to be potty trained. He knows how, and when, and he doesn't show signs of being afraid. Sometimes, he goes by himself. Sometimes he goes with encouragement. But most of the time he refuses.

I've tried punishment, and quickly gave that up, as it made things worse. I've tried sweets, stickers, cars and toys as rewards. I've tried praise, hugs and kisses. Nothing so far has motivated him for more than a few days. He only seems to care that he is wet about half the time. If you have any ideas, please tell me.

Louis' mother has many of the same difficulties as Betsy's mother above (although the issue has gone on even longer), and I would ask her the same questions. But I include her email as well because it's a great example of inconsistency. Whenever someone tells me they've 'tried everything' (including punishment, in this case), it usually means that they haven't stayed with one approach long enough to give it a chance to work. What's probably happening in this case is that, the moment Louis has an accident, Mum changes the rules.

First, Louis' mother has to choose one method and stick with it no matter what happens. She also has to take control of the process. As it is now, her three-and-a-half-year-old son has the reins. He sees her frustration. He knows how to get her to react – to cajole, to reward, to praise – and he's become empowered by it.

Second, she has to put Louis in underpants (she doesn't say, but I'll bet he's in pull-ups). Then she should use the timer method just as I advised Betsy's mother. She has to take care not to schedule trips to the bathroom to coincide with an activity – he's less likely to cooperate if interrupted.

She should also put him in charge of the dressing and undressing.

A note on 'punishing' a child: it never works and it often creates really serious problems in the future, such as fear of the toilet and bed-wetting. Moreover, by the time a child is Louis' age, the real world will be punishment enough. At his age, most children are toilet trained. It won't be long before some of Louis' playmates comment on his dirty or wet pants. Mum shouldn't add to his humiliation, or point out that 'other children' (good children) use the toilet or that they don't need to wear pull-ups any more.

'Two Years Old and Suddenly Afraid of the Toilet'

My two-year-old daughter, Kayla, was doing great in the potty department. She was dry for several weeks during the day, and then she suddenly became afraid of the toilet. I don't know what happened. I work three days a week, and we have a wonderful nanny who comes in when I'm at the office. Is this common?

Kayla's mother has to respect her daughter's fear, and also figure out where it came from. When things have been going smoothly, and suddenly a child becomes afraid of the toilet, it's almost always because something happened. **Has she been constipated lately?** If so, and she pushed a little too hard one day, she might now associate that discomfort with the toilet. Just to be sure, I would suggest increasing the fibre in her diet – sweetcorn, peas, whole grains, prunes, fruit. Also increase her liquid intake.

What kind of seat do you use? If it's an add-on seat, maybe Kayla wasn't held properly one day and started slipping through, or perhaps the seat wasn't on securely and shook when Kayla got on or off. If it was a free-standing potty, maybe it tipped. **Do you use a stool underfoot?** Without one, Kayla might have felt insecure.

Because Kayla's mother is not the only one to handle toilet training, I would also ask about the nanny. **Did you take the time to explain your plan – better yet, to write it down – and to show your nanny exactly what to do?** If your child is in someone else's care during the day, it's important to make sure they know exactly what you're doing and carry out your toilet-training plan when you're not there. **Did you include information about what you do when Kayla pees or poos**

in her pants? It's also important to assess attitudes, especially if your childcare provider is from another country. Some people ridicule children or even smack them when they poo in their pants. Granted, it's sometimes hard to figure out exactly what went on in your absence, but these are all possibilities that you might (tactfully) explore.

When a child is afraid, we have to respect her fears. Mum can ask Kayla, 'Can you tell Mummy what you're scared of?' Once she finds out how her daughter's fear started (from Kayla or her other enquiries), Mum has to go back to the basics: read one or more children's books about using the toilet. Go to the toilet with Kayla and give her a choice: 'Do you want to go before Mummy, or should I do it first?' When you take a child to the toilet with you, she gets to see that there's nothing threatening about it.

If all else fails, Mum could see if Kayla was willing to sit on her lap when she's on the toilet and have Kayla go between her legs. Until her fear diminishes, Mum could act like a human training seat. Kayla is not likely to get dependent on her mother. Two-year-olds want to be 'big kids' and, as soon as the fear dissipates, Kayla will want to go to the toilet on her own.

Sometimes children develop a fear of public toilets. In that case, make sure that your child empties her bladder before leaving home and try to take short excursions while you're in the training phase. If you're doing local errands, arrange to stop at another mum's house en route.

'Got a Good Start and Then Regressed'

> I thought my son Eric was well on his way to being toilet trained, but when we moved to our new house he started putting up a fight every time I wanted him to go to the toilet. What did I do wrong?

How close to your move did you start toilet training? Eric's mum may have a case of bad timing on her hands. It is never advisable to start toilet training too close to a big family change such as a move or a new baby, or when the child himself is in the middle of any kind of transition – for example, teething or just after an illness.

Is anything else new happening at home? Toilet training can also be interrupted by parents' arguments, a new nanny, or if something else is happening at home or in a playgroup that's upsetting to the child.

Go back to the basics, and start your toilet-training plan from the beginning.

'Missed the Window and Now We're in for a Battle'

Sadie showed several signs of readiness between 17 and 20 months, but I put it off because Baby #2 was coming. Sadie was really ready, and actually went on the potty a few times, voluntarily, when #2 was a newborn. But #2 was such an awful handful that I didn't have the mental or physical energy to put into it. So now I have to wait until she decides that she wants to, or get tough and have a traumatic fight with her.

I respect Sadie's mother's honesty, and that she knew training too close to a big family change wasn't a good idea. But she also has potty panic, and that's preventing her from seeing her other options.

Sadie first started showing signs at 17 months. Had her mum stuck with it at that point – before the second baby arrived – Sadie might have been trained.

Sadie is now over two and, while it is harder to initiate training at this point, especially with a new baby in the house, there are other solutions besides getting 'tough' or having a 'traumatic fight' with her daughter. Sadie is obviously ready to learn and can communicate with her mother. I would suggest that Mum implements my plan: take a week simply to observe Sadie's elimination patterns and to talk about toilet habits with Sadie. Make a point of taking Sadie to the toilet with her. Also take Sadie on a shopping expedition for big-girl underpants.

When it's time to commence toilet training, Mum will change the baby a few minutes before she thinks her older daughter might need to go on the loo. She will involve Sadie in the process: 'Would you like to help Mummy change the baby?' Give Sadie a little step stool so she can get closer and let her hold the nappy, the cream and feel like a little assistant.

Mum also might casually point out to her older child, 'You don't need nappies any more because you know how to go on the toilet like I do. As soon as I change the baby's nappy, let's you and I go to the bathroom together.' If she allows Sadie to participate, times her bathroom trips well, and gives her choices ('Do you want to go first, or should Mummy?'), she's much less likely to get into a power struggle with Sadie.

'Three-Year-Old Only Pretends to Go in the Potty and Then Does It in Her Nappy'

Amy will sit on the potty and pretend to go, but never does. She wears big-girl underpants but, when she has to go potty, she announces, 'I need a nappy, please,' and goes into the nappy. We spoke with our doctor about this and he says that obviously Amy CAN go on the potty because she has control enough to wait for a nappy. He said not to push her to go on the potty – the more we push, the more she will insist on doing it her way. This is hard for us as we also have a seven-year-old who was potty trained very easily. I'm afraid, with Amy, her will is stronger than mine.

Another mother on my website suggested giving Amy a nappy but cutting a hole in it, so that she could be wearing the nappy and go on the toilet. There are some children who have trouble literally letting go of their bowels. And a hole in the nappy might help in that case.

However, Amy is three years old, a very smart and independent child. The fact that Mum says that Amy's 'will is stronger than mine', tells me that toilet drama is not the only battle going on in this household. I would ask, **Are you**

having power struggles in other arenas? If so, Amy has found one new way to manipulate her family – not an unusual trick for a younger child.

My approach would be to get rid of all the nappies in the house and tell Amy that you're doing it. When she asks for a nappy, remind her, 'I can't give you one. We don't have any left. Let's go to the toilet instead.' I can understand a doctor saying not to push when a child is two, but, at three, I'm sceptical. Some children need a little shove, and I suspect that Amy is one of them.

'He Uses His Penis Like a Fire Hose'

Of course he does! It goes with the territory. Indeed, toilet training a boy is often a case of 'be careful what you wish for – you just might get it'. Even training boys to pee sitting down at first doesn't necessarily solve the problem. Once boys get the knack of using their penises, they're especially fond of target practice.

One father made the most of it and sped up his son's training in the process, by putting Cheerios in the toilet bowl and telling him to aim at them. If his son missed, he cleaned it up. Another mother trained her sons and daughters without a potty or a child-sized seat altogether facing backwards on the toilet seat.

'She Wants to Pee Standing Up'

Especially if she's seen Dad or an older brother peeing, you can't blame her. You just have to be patient and explain, this is how girls pee and that's how boys pee. Show her. At worst, let her try, but warn her that, if it doesn't end up in the toilet, she'll have to clean it up. Usually the sensation of pee running down her leg is all that it takes to nip this habit in the bud.

'Have Trouble Getting Her Off the Potty'

My daughter showed a huge interest in potty training at 18 months, so we started. Unfortunately, it was wintertime and, between getting sick and my having a newborn to care for, we started and stopped a few times and finally stopped. She is now almost 23 months old and we are thinking about starting again. I realise now that we made a few grave errors initially: starting, stopping, letting her sit on the potty for an hour to read books.

My question is, do other children give parents a hard time about getting off the potty after three minutes? I have a feeling that my daughter will again, and I want to be better prepared this time. Previously, she wouldn't want to get off, and it would end up in a battle, which I didn't want associated with potty training, so I would let her sit on the potty for as long as she wanted. Any advice on how to get her off without an argument?

The first thing I'd suggest is a timer. Especially at 23 months, you can say, 'When the bell rings, we have to check for pee and poo.' If there's none in the toilet, say, 'That was a good try – we can come back later and try again.'

But there's a bigger issue here as well. This mother bent over backwards to avoid a power struggle – she says, over toilet training. But I'll bet that she's backing down in other arenas as well.

Epilogue

Many of the problems I see result from too-late toilet training. If your child is not trained by the age of four, seek the help of your doctor or a paediatric urologist to make sure that physical problems aren't impeding his progress. This is rare, though.

One mum, whose son was not trained at three, told me that her doctor eased her anxiety by telling her to look around her. 'He asked if I knew any adults who were still in nappies!' He was correct. Remember that most children are trained . . . eventually. Some can actually manage the feat in a few days, because they're ready and their parents are willing to put aside everything and just concentrate on this one important task. Others will take a year or longer.

If you ask a thousand experts out there, you'll probably find a thousand variations on toilet training that span the continuum from tackling toilet training a few months after birth to waiting until the child decides. Read up on all the methods, and pick and choose a plan that seems suitable for your baby and your lifestyle. Talk to other parents and find out what worked for them.

Whatever method you choose, lighten up. Laugh about it. The less anxiety you have, the better chance your child has of succeeding.

Pearls of Wisdom from Those Who've Been There, Done That

Here are a series of titbits from the real frontline warriors themselves: mothers who are in the process of or have completed toilet training.

- Do not nag, nag, nag your child about going to the toilet. We never pushed our daughter in any way, but we gave her lots of praise and encouragement for her successes.

- I highly recommend *The Potty Book for Girls/Boys*, which helps get the message across and which we parents find entertaining as well.

- Don't start when you have a big life event coming up – a new baby, going to day care, company, travelling even for a weekend. It throws everything out of whack, and you take three big steps backwards each time.

- You can leave them naked if you want, but I just have a feeling that they will pee on your floor and then feel ashamed.

- Remember that your child is an individual, and, if you make her feel comfortable and in control of the situation (even though you are secretly controlling it), then you are more likely to get positive results.

- Remember you are learning to toilet train as much as your child is learning to be trained. Don't be too hard on yourself if you make a few mistakes along the way.

- It won't go as smoothly in real life as it sounds like it will by reading the books. But, then again, did your pregnancy? Your delivery? Breastfeeding?

- Don't stress about getting it done in a certain amount of time. Learning to walk was a process with many false starts, and toilet training is, too.

- Don't tell anyone you are toilet training or they will bug you every day with criticism and 'helpful advice'. Wait until the process is all done and then make a big announcement about your child's great accomplishment. The exception to this is if you have a wonderfully supportive community like www.babywhisperer.com where you can share your successes and frustrations and people will respond with encouragement and *actual* help.

Index

Also available from Vermilion

Top Tips from the Baby Whisperer

Handy tips on everything from feeding
and bathing to choosing a carer and
teaching your baby to sleep.

Price: £6.99   ISBN: 9780091917449

Top Tips from the Baby Whisperer for Toddlers

Quick tips on everything from discipline
and socialising to potty-training and
fostering independence in your toddler.

Price £6.99   ISBN: 9780091917432

Order titles direct from www.rbooks.co.uk/babywhisperer

Also available from Vermilion

Top Tips from the Baby Whisperer: Sleep

Handy tips from Tracy Hogg's practical sleep programme to help you overcome your baby's sleep problems.

Price: £6.99   ISBN: 9780091929725

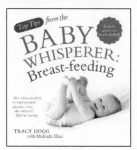

Top Tips from the Baby Whisperer: Breast-feeding

Easy quick advice for solving common feeding issues in the first six months and moving on to solid foods. Also addresses bottle-feeding.

Price £6.99   ISBN: 9780091929732

Order titles direct from www.rbooks.co.uk/babywhisperer